A ROLE FOR ARTISTS
IN TROUBLED TIMES

Ways to Think About Making Art
Ways for Artists to Find an Audience
Renewing Humanity Through Art

by Robert Golden

Cover Design & Photo by Robert Golden

Published by WriteSideLeft Ltd, UK
www.writesideleft.com

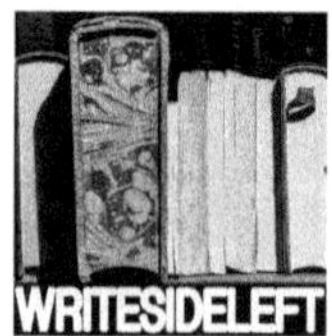

By The Author

DOCUMENTARY WORK
• The *People Working Series*
10 books published by Kestrel- Penguin
• *Down The Road*
published by The Writers and Readers Publishing Cooperative
• *Home*
published by Robert Golden Pictures
• *Simple Things*
published by Robert Golden Pictures
a monograph of his still-life work

THE ARTS
• *Filling The Box* parts 1 and 2
published online at https://www.robertgoldenpictures.com/
• *Inside Outside*
about of the movement director, Monika Plagneux
at https://www.robertgoldenpictures.com/

NOVEL
• *A Forgettable Man*
published by Writesideleft

POETRY
Windows Kiss The Shadows Of The Passing Thirty Million
published by Triarchy Press
https://www.triarchypress.net/windows-kiss.html

for Odette and Imogen,
and all the children and all the artists

"I can't run no more with that lawless crowd
while the killers in high places
say their prayers out loud"
from Leonard Cohen's Anthem

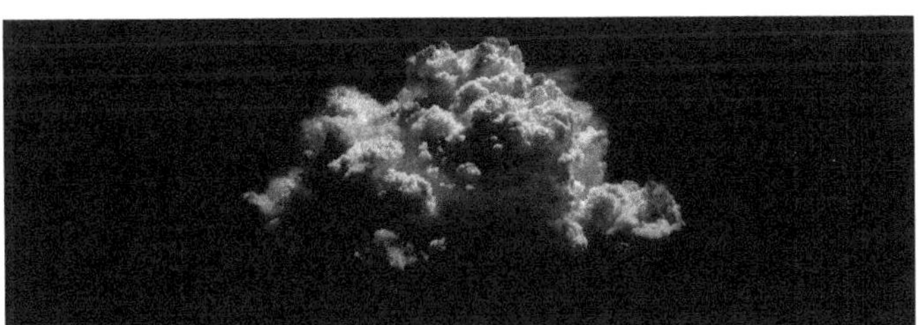

Clouds between Beirut and London, 2010;
photograph Robert Golden

CONTENTS

Introduction

1
Pictures, Purpose and Presence
A visual autobiography
2
Process
A way to discover themes and subject matter
3
Underlying Assumptions
4
**A Role For Artists
In Troubled Times**
5
A Dream

Biographical Notes

Footnotes

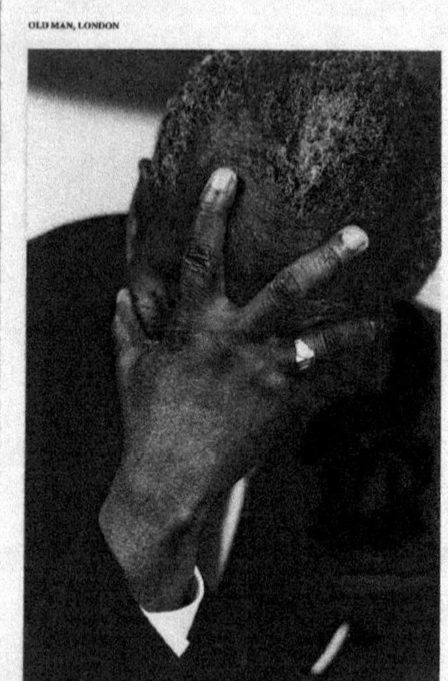

Panel from an exhibition about black people's lives in England in the 1970's; photograph/text: Robert Golden

INTRODUCTION

For artists surrounded by our hollowed-out culture
to be able to create for a socially progressive,
hungry-eyed audience while making a living
and not being ignored and forgotten
we share a struggle.

Over the years I have worked as a photographer and film-maker, and via my history of publishing and encountering agents, publishers, producers and editors, (see biographical notes) I have learned that what I have to say is contradictory, not to the proclaimed but to the actual values of Anglo-American middle class cultural and political practices[i].

From what I have witnessed as well as researched, I have come to understand that capitalism is now practiced in the most injurious way for the majority of people and that democracy has been profoundly undermined by the ultra-rich who purchase politicians and political parties and then bend them to their demands rather than to representing the wishes of the electorate. Since the early 1980's, they have purposely transformed our culture, morality, ethics, wishes and our art. In so doing, they have stolen hope, especially from our bewildered young. They have in part accomplished these changes by increased centralized control of educational institutions, and increased media monopolization of popular culture and the news.

The Establishment[ii] has guardians at the gates of all these institutions who control what does and does not get taught, made, seen or distributed. Every truth-speaking journalist, film-maker, visual artist and writer faces the difficulty of making a living and finding an audience without the support of the electronic and print media.

Recently a French academic, Mathilde Bertrand[iii], wrote about my position earlier in my life:

> *"In the small world of British photography in the late 1970s, Camerawork[iv] acted as an essential forum for the exchange of ideas between photographers, art critics and theoreticians with an interest in photography. It published articles by theoreticians John Berger, John Tagg and Victor Burgin, giving the magazine intellectual rigor, and made room for polemical tribunes, which in turn led to heated discussions. For instance, Spence's interview with American photographer Robert Golden triggered an important debate. (Spence 1976) Golden's radical conception of documentary photography in the class struggle, his call for photographers to reflect on their class position and on the political determinations and effects of their images, pointed to the moral duty of the photographer."*

Still today I believe more than ever it is the moral duty of photographers, journalists, artists and intellectuals to confront power.

In creative work, as in the rest of human endeavour, there are many ways to accomplish those things art and artists can achieve. What I offer is one that has served me and which may make sense to you.

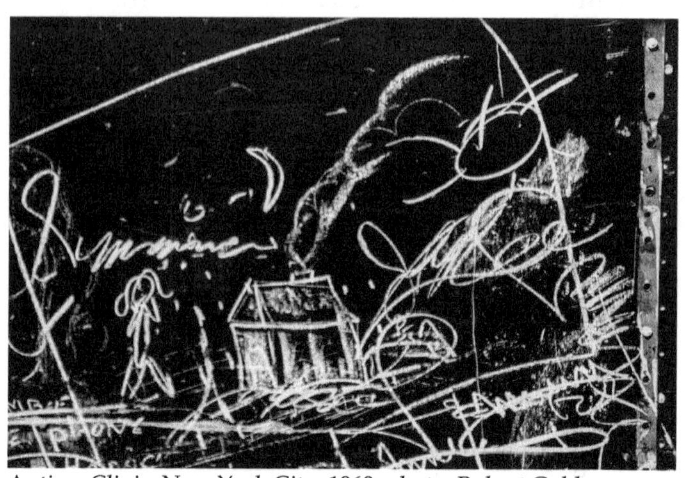

Autism Clinic, New York City, 1968, photo: Robert Golden

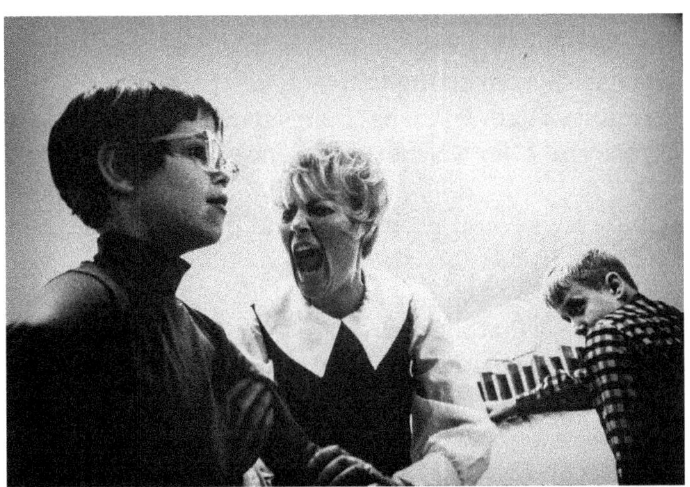

Teacher 'treats' autistic child, New York, 1967;
photograph: Robert Golden

1
PICTURES, PURPOSE AND PRESENCE
A VISUAL AUTOBIOGRAPHY OF A PHOTOGRAPHER/FILM-MAKER

In the following essay it is vital that readers see the images I am referring to during the course of reading. That way, what I am saying will make more sense and offer a richer experience.

There are several problems about printing these pictures in the published book.

The first is that the charges to purchase permission for image usage are high, thus, by necessity, pushing this volume's price up.

The second is that some universities who are in possession of certain photographer's works will not respond to requests.

The third is that at the moment it is not possible to obtain a high standard of four-colour reproduction for published work on the Internet, at least at a reasonable price.

With these limitations in mind I have provided, at the appropriate places in the texts, two ways of viewing the references. There are my own images and those of the painter Ricky Romain that are accessible here:

https://vimeo.com/301462319

This will take you to a film you can start and stop
before and after each section. Use SEE 1 for instance
(the number) with a short description. Go to the
URL and keep it open as you read. That way you
can hit the button and the images will play. With
some there is accompanying music, which, should
you wish, just turn off.

The second group are noted in the text as FIND xx.
The essential key words are given to help you
Google the correct image.

This essay is mainly about photography and the
fine arts, but it is also about life becoming richer
when we are compelled by the beauty and
empathy of the fine arts, films, photographs,
poetry, music and novels to look into the souls of
others.

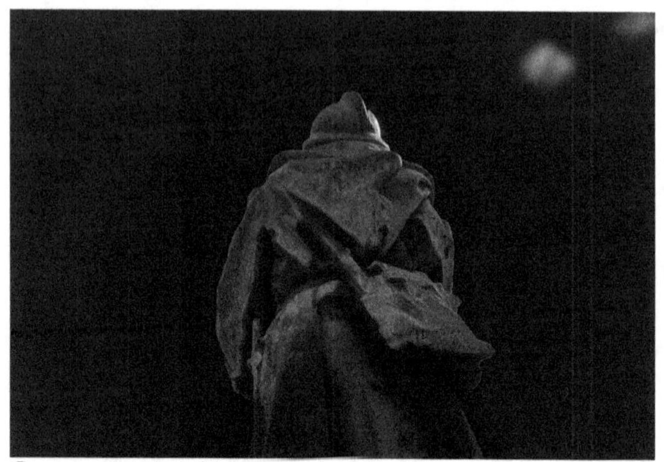

Commemoration, Sarteano Italy, March 2016;
photograph: Robert Golden

INTRODUCTION

I'm going to take you on a journey of images; images that transformed me from being a kid living in a home with no regard for art and with no books nor ideas to discuss, into a person whose entire adult existence has been dedicated to making photographs and films. As you will come to understand, my dedication has not been to photography and film-making, but to using them as tools to make sense of life. I have become what I am because I was rescued by culture and by pictures in particular.

I'm not saying that how I understand the following images would be validated by academic research. I'm only telling you what I made of the pictures and how the pictures affected me. I hope, in explaining my experiences, you may see that I have tried to turn away from suffocating cultural/social and political attitudes, from sexism and macho nationalism, from racism and the hatred of those who are different, while turning towards ways of thinking which ask questions about who I wished to be and what my responsibilities to others should be and in particular, what my responsibilities with a camera in hand should be.

Consciously or not, we have all been raised within a culture affected by, and in part formed by great artist's images. Their attitudes, which have become a part of our collective visual understanding, have also affected my development and my work. This visual language, like all languages, helps us to know who we are and how to discover truths beyond the surrounding, swamping Anglo/American popular cultures. In other words, my photographs, have inherited, not their genius, but a fragment of the artist's humane worldview.

SEE 1: images from earlier in my life.
https://vimeo.com/301462319
 (This URL is for all of the 'SEE' images.)

SEE 2: images from 30 to 40 years later.

You will have noticed that my pictures are not high dynamic range, chocolate box coloured photos of fireworks against starry skies. They are simple images. You may see they are united by a particular visual sensibility. Before I continue I want to relate two quick stories

DIEGO RIVERA'S DETROIT MURAL

When I was 8 years old, I was offered special drawing and painting classes in the Detroit Institute of Art. On the second Saturday I attended, we children were shown into a high narrow room that had a painted story. It continued from wall to wall and on two sides from floor to ceiling created by the famous Mexican post- revolutionary muralist painter, Diego Rivera.

FIND: Diego+Rivera+Detroit+Industrial+Mural+Art+Institute +of+Detroit

I thought the whole world was in that huge mural. The walls vibrated with life flowing out of the earth to the farmers and workers. I sensed everything was connected: from the soil to the roots of plants to the weather which nurtured them; from the farmers who harvested the food to the women who pounded

the maize to bake the bread; from the women's
bread to the miners who dug the coal and pig iron;
from the sailors on the ships who transported the
minerals to the mills that coked the iron ore; from
the men who pressed and punched the steel into cars
that produced the owner's profits; to the priest and
the wealthy who owned and disdained the workers.
Everything had a meaning and everything was
interrelated. I thought all of life was described
within the mural.

The teacher explained that after it had been viewed
by local business and religious leaders, they
demanded the painting be covered over because it
was Marxist propaganda. But, said the teacher, *"to
his lasting credit the museum's curator, Wilhelm
Valentiner, refused to allow that to happen"*.

After I had been introduced to that mural I knew I
needed to be some sort of visual artist. Because of
that experience, I never had to be convinced that all
children need to be exposed to all the arts.

DISCOVERING PHOTOGRAPHY

Two years later I opened the pages of a
commemorative annual published by Life Magazine.
I turned the pages, looking at the ads for cars,
cookies and refrigerators and came across a set of
photographs that took my breath away. They were
in rich black and white, glowing off the smooth
semi-glossy pages. Picture after picture showed, in
an almost three-dimensional sharpness, the effects of
war on American soldiers from the battle for the
Pacific in 1945.

FIND: W+Eugene+Smith+War+in+the+Pacific

I saw that the photographer was called W. Eugene Smith and that he was, as I, born in the Midwest. Once again my world was altered. Diego Rivera's museum mural, my continual amazement with the look, beauty and effects of light; my childhood dream of life having meaning; my childish wish to achieve a heroic something; all these unclear desires fused in Smith's photographs: Smith from the Midwest; Smith with only a camera in hand.

LEONARDO DA VINCI'S PORTRAITS

Now to truly begin this journey I want to tell you about my encounter with Leonardo Da Vinci's portraits. Look first at Leonardo Da Vinci's St Anne and Family.

FIND: leonardo+da+vinci+portrait+st+anne

Now look at these icon painting of about the same period.

FIND: Icon+painting+15th+century

Leonardo was born in 1452, in the middle of the Italian Renaissance, during a period when icon paintings like those I just referred you to were still a dominant mode of picture making.[v]

In those pre-renaissance medieval icons, neither an individual's characteristics, nor an individual's psychology, nor distinctive attitudes and emotions, nor the trials of life are present on the icon's generalised faces and bodies; because for the Judaeo Christian God there is no important human presence in God's infinite time. So the reflections of God in people are like cartoons rather than people themselves that we can recognise. They are all simply a reflection of the Holy Spirit.

The importance of an individual as a being separate from the spirit of God was, previous to the Renaissance, unimaginable.

When Leonardo painted his utterly physical, emotionally charged portraits, it became clear he was no longer obeying the God centred demands of the church, but embracing the human centred consciousness of the Renaissance.

He and others liberated Europeans from centuries of mysticism. He helped re-centre consciousness away from a holy spirit into the individual human being. Renaissance means 're-birth' which was precisely what it was – a rebirth of the spirit and acknowledgement of the being and value of the individual so movingly revealed by the 2nd century BC Greeks in their philosophy, theatre and visual arts.

While having seen these images, I was growing up surrounded by a thousand mistruths, fragments of belief in a mythical god, and buried in a morass of gift card-emotions and unformulated social theories. For me as a young person to recognise that Leonardo, 500 years earlier, saw through the falsehoods of his own period, opened my eyes to the cultural fog I was being brought up in.

I learned that art crosses the boundaries of culture and time.

After discovering these things in Leonardo, I wished to rid myself of religious and socially imposed illusions so that I too could see - without the fog of heaven and hell - truths about events, people and things in front of my camera; to discover a common recognizable humanity between myself and others rather than to make-do with superficial photographs or worse, to impose, through my photographs my ego-centric teenage self-preoccupations on other people.

Leonardo helped me to understand that there was a profound difference between recording light reflecting off objects - like those luminous flatly lit icons, and capturing the human spirit within what appeared to be real flesh and blood. This led me to understand that forms of art that rely upon the precise look of the material world, that is – on the verifiable surface of reality - often offer only a shallow representation of that reality.

When I first saw Leonardo's drawings, their beauty, along with my admiration for black and white films and photographs, led me to photograph mostly in black and white.

I recognised that if colour does not serve to strengthen the composition or if it does not help to tell the story of the picture, it has no reason to be there; it's then just superficial decoration.

Monochrome allows me to emphasise the structures and volumes in a picture, as well as an enhancement of drama and a concentration on what is important. In other words – I can better reveal the underlying forms by ridding the image of superficial colour details.

SEE: 3 Ian Ritchie portrait - digital negative to reduced colour to monochrome.

In the transformation above you saw the digital negative as it was downloaded from the camera, then the first stage of editing and finally the image reduced to pure monochrome.

From my point of view I am not reporting, I am evoking. The so-called 'naturalism of colour' is meaningless to me.

For me then a young photographer, a non-believer with little patience for religion, the lifefulness and the beauty of Da Vinci's images honoured not a God, but rather human love and kindness between people.

His drawings and painting affected me in the way Renaissance humanism affected Western culture: he sensitized me to the distinctiveness of other's souls – his pictures shaped my empathy as they educated me visually, and, as I said earlier, he helped me to see 'so called 'truths' or 'common knowledge' are a product of one's time and place rather than some god or state-given supposed fixed reality.

Da Vinci of course affected my thoughts about photography but as he enriched my life with the beauty and empathy of his work he encouraged me, a naive teenager, to look into the souls of others rather than to see people as types, or specimens of class or conditions, as in these early pictures of mine.

SEE 4: Caring for Strangers

EDWARD WESTON

When I was 15 and looking continually at photographers' images I had come across Edward Weston's sinuous if not to say sexual peppers and conch shells.

FIND: Edward+Weston+peppers

FIND: Edward+Weston+nautilus+shells

Then I came across a close-up of a cabbage leaf by Weston.

FIND: Edward+Weston+cabbage

The picture stunned me because the leaf itself was flawed and not inherently beautiful, yet the photograph is. The light glowing off of the receding ribs, the composition of the leaf running towards the camera, the gloomy sensuous tones compelled me to return to it over and over in my life. For me, I imagined the richness of his simple existence. I could smell his studio on a hot California morning; I could feel the day and the breeze through his screen door. Quietly, to myself, I can only say, 'this is very beautiful'.

It sings not only about the sinuous structures of the organic world, a world more honest and yes, more down to earth than our social world; but it sings as well about how his humble yet rich imagination had been brought to an otherwise unnoticed leaf of a common vegetable and turned it into an aesthetic pleasure.

How much does that sing about human potential? Weston's cabbage granted me hopes and dreams – these intellectual and emotional gifts of art that provided me possibilities for a transformation of my own character in what was and is, in too many parts of the Anglo/American world, a wilderness of people who not only have no hope, but also have no hope of having hope.

In my mid teens, the influences of Da Vinci, Weston and others mingled with the rest of my life's slowly acquired learning and experiences and then one day I realized all of my work and learning were leading me to my own slowly evolving definable voice.

Amongst other things, Weston helped me to understand it was not just the social world I should photograph, but I should allow myself to embrace this beautiful planet and the wonderful things we as a species have made, as these:

SEE 5: Embracing the earth: (Positano San Gimigniano)

But Weston's published journals, called his DAYBOOKS, introduced me to the idea of art having social significance. I was learning, through photography, about egalitarianism, about an ideal world, and about the importance of art, beauty and ideas that were beyond the surrounding empty popular culture I survived within.

Through Weston's photographs I fell in love with his lover, Tina Modotti – a heroic, self-sacrificing, talented and gorgeous woman. That admiration overcame any ideas that men were superior to women.

FIND: edward+weston+portraits+tina+modotti+on+terrace

I identified that there was in Weston's images something vital, attractive, and necessary for me.

He helped me appreciate that 'developing clarity about the world was primary to being able to photograph it; and that there was a direct relationship between who I was, how I felt about things and the photographs I would make.

I saw, in his deep focused images, a respect and love of each person and thing in the frame.

FIND: edward+weston+landscapes

His ability to transform simple structures or natural objects into powerful images, to create potent, and solid compositions with a sinuous distribution of tones continually inspired me.

For all the realism of the deep sharpness of his images, his rendering of tones is expressive rather than descriptive. This is the point: for all the objectively descriptive nature of his images, his photographs are of his internal disposition – this intense poetic reality of 'being' rather than of the surface of 'things'.

These pictures of mine inherit an appreciation of Weston.

SEE 6: An Inheritance from Edward Weston (Matera, Piazza in Positano and soldier, Sarteano)

Making photographs was assuming a role greater than them being simply a descriptive tool; it was becoming an expressive, poetic medium for me. I began to understand that I wanted to make rather than to take pictures.

I began to understand all the more about the sanctity of objects and people and how they could be enhanced through technique, how composition and light help to evoke emotions, and how the repetitions and the chaos of form offered me command over the wildness of a messy natural and social world.

More importantly, I was beginning to think that I too could live life for truth and beauty, and although I was not then sure of their value for others, they were becoming a reality for me.

As I matured politically and aesthetically, I realized that beauty was not an entertaining attachment to life. Although I may have existed only with sufficient food and warmth, without beauty I would have had a hole in my soul. Without beauty, who would I have become, what would I have been? How then would I differ from the sexism of the football jocks, the gung-ho militarism of the junior officers training corps, from the racism of the kids who had been taught to hate knowledge and learning? Was art and culture giving me a reason to exist? Was it defining who I was?

MICHELANGELO'S SLAVES

I want to share with you some thoughts about Michelangelo's eight Slave sculptures, sometimes called the Prisoners, which can be seen in Florence.

To me, the first one, called Awakening Slave implied several things.

FIND: michelangelo+slaves+or+prisoners

The struggle to tear himself out of the stone led me to understand my need to liberate myself from my surrounding social/political and economic constraints which I came to see controlled my thinking and the boundaries of my future. These constraints were always apparent in any exchange with bureaucrats, teachers, parents and my peer's social attitudes. These constraints of laws, rules, habits and manners seeped deep into the social norms, the popular culture and indeed into my family's life.

In the simplest way, I began to understand those who entrapped me in their 'normal world' were shadows in front of my lenses, obscuring the truths of the world. The slave's struggle personalised for me my efforts to obey my own inclinations and to become what I wished to be, even in the face of hostility.

They taught me that I wanted to become a 'mensch'
– a word that in German means 'to be a man', but in
Yiddish it means 'to be filled with humanity'.

Perhaps through the heroes of my young life –
Martin Luther King, Mohammed Ali, through
Ghandi and later Mandela, through the
photographers and poets and novelists I viewed and
read and the things I had done - to wish to become a
mensch seemed necessary. The concept linked for
me my desire to understand the world and people
with my need to define who I was and what I
wished to be, while explaining to myself my
opposition to what I saw as a macho, supposedly
manly but vulgar and ignoble world of men.

The Slaves posed other questions to me. How could
I, an average person, produce work that could speak
to other human beings? How could I commit my
skills to create a better world? Indeed, how could
light passing through my lenses affect other's
consciousness, as had the many pictures that
affected my view of life?

Remembering the rough hewn stone against the
slave's partly exposed finely polished flesh showed
me I needed to develop skills and craftsmanship;
and that I needed to learn the history of my medium
so as not to attempt to reinvent the wheel.

Meanwhile I had been introduced to the novels of
Andre Malraux (*Man's Fate* about freewill), to Jean
Paul Sartre (*Nausea* about the nature of existence in a
rotten world and his *Being And Nothingness* about
the nature of human life and the limits of freedom),

and especially to Albert Camus (*The Stranger* and *The Plague)* about the absurdity and tragedy of human life, and to *The Myth Of Sisyphus* in which Camus finds - in recognizing the potential dignity of life through people's unstoppable struggle for freedom, one can overcome life's inherently absurd and tragic nature.

To me, a diligent, intellectually hungry but humourless young person, a part of Camus' brilliance was to write *"that while our psyche wishes to survive, our bodies are destined to die"*.

All of these worked on my young and slowly maturing mind as I struggled to overcome my dark view of life – its venality, small-mindedness, its ugliness, people's disregard of beauty, poetry and lofty ideals, and, for me to assemble a way to embrace my passion for living and indeed my lust for life – for making images, for making a meaningful life, and for making love.

Perhaps most importantly, recalling the struggle of the Slaves, I had to come to understand the differences between art that serves those who rule history and art that serves the victims of that history.

I instinctively understood that I must come to discover the differences between serving wealth and serving truth. In so doing, I discovered the difference between art and commercial art, between art and propaganda; between helping oppress, or helping liberate other's imaginations.

I came to understand the differences between creating work that addresses people's needs from works of decoration and entertainment that either ignore those needs or reinforce the ideas of the status quo.

I'm not saying I had come to complete resolutions about all of these things, nor indeed that I could even articulate them as I can now, but rather, these were the ideas I continually tussled with.

For reasons I will not belabour you, across many years I shot pictures like this to make a living:

SEE 7: commercial still life

Eventually I was able to turn my back on commercialism. Here are more recent photographs.

SEE 8: Recent photographs

Do the later ones seem quieter, less obvious, perhaps in relation to the graphics of the first few pictures they seem visually dull?

The still-lives are meant to seduce you into buying something; the documentary images are meant to encourage you to ask questions.

The still-lives come from the offerings of street vendors; the documentary images come from what? An artist? A journalist? A truth-teller?

The still-lives want your money; the documentary images want your emotional and intellectual engagement.

At some point in my young life I discovered in Ernest Hemingway's novel, *The Old Man And The Sea* that a particular struggle, for instance a group of people's hatred of another group, or in the case of his novel, a fight with a fish may be turned into a trial of human endurance and of human goodness. I was beginning to catch a glimpse of metaphor.

The sculptor Giacometti wrote, *"looking is an interrogation of the absolute"*. That says 'artists must always be curious', a curiosity which at the worst of times, is condemned by the authorities as detrimental to public order.

I began to understand why the hierarchies who dominate my life have only contempt for artists unless they can decorate their palaces, entertain them, or effectively communicate their ideologically tilted messages to the rest of society.

It led me to understand that propaganda is a one-sided proclamation that demands unquestioning acceptance of the message, whereas art encourages enquiry and a dialogue.

If before the "making" there is contemplation and discovery, artists may transform trivia by their gaze and skill into a contemplation of history - of power, wealth or poverty, of gods or holy spirits, of certainty or confusion, or of being and nothingness. All of this I learned from Michelangelo's slaves.

PAUL STRAND

Through the photographer Paul Strand's portrayal of cultures around the world, his work stood as an example for me of how the universality of humanity could be revealed in photographs. He made photo-essays in the northeast of the US, in Ghana, Egypt, Italy and other places.

He used a large format stills camera sitting on a wooden tripod, of course shooting on film.

In his essays he pictured three things: broad land and cityscapes, mid shots of objects used in everyday life and at times close-ups of nature, and wide to close-up portraits of individuals or groups in their habitats.

FIND: paul+strand+landscape

He offered up an un-romanticized view of the day-by-day reality of the cultures he photographed. The images rang of truth and directness and they were beautifully crafted.

In his books there were never pools of detail-less black ink or glaring paper-white holes, but a continuous silvery fusion of tones from deepest grey to detailed whites.

For all the differences of wealth, race, clothing, occupations and so on, everyone, from every country was pictured with dignity and somehow that dignity created joy in me.

I grew up in a racist home in a racist community
filled with hatred for the very people photographed
with dignity by Strand. His pictures convinced me
that he, Strand –a stranger to me, a man far older
then me - was right, and yes, that I too was right and
my brother and father and uncles and all the rest
had somehow been stricken by a delirium of
superiority.

For me to try to understand truths unacceptable to
those around me was proving socially
uncomfortable. It was making me even more of an
outsider. That's probably why Malraux, Sartre and
Camus appealed to me, because as Strand assured
me that my instincts about the insanity of racism
were right, those authors validated for me my desire
to continue trying to make sense of life outside the
norms which surrounded me.

A Paul Strand collection of images, as *Un Paese*,
photographs in the Po River Valley in Northern Italy
is clear, certain of itself and offers a calmness in its
careful observations. It's like looking at crystal on a
bright but overcast day.

Because his photographs appeared emotionally calm
on the surface they seemed almost ethnographic.
This encouraged me to accept something I wanted –
my young intellectual and emotional interests could
add up to truth telling.

His work also helped me to understand the
differences between the narrative aspects of
photographs and the visual qualities of
photographs, that is, between the story and the

picture's forms. The ability to see this truly helped me to grasp that I would need to understand the relationship between form and content, and how technique plays a role in fusing them together.

This was a revelation for my picture making and my visual storytelling abilities.

I began to read in his photographs how individuals, groups, land and cityscapes and the tools of work explained the way a community survives by making and re-making itself everyday. He helped me to understand the value of the series, the essay and the story.

I began to understand the need to establish the sense of a particular place; to photograph the emotional disposition of people rather than only their function or actions; to concern myself with the compositions and the quality of light in each image; to recognize the way an essay's internal rhythm is established by the close-up, the mid-shot and the wide-shot; to also regard the flow of emotions as storytelling elements, binding themes such as time, tone, processes, and life itself from birth to death, and to be able to appreciate the contribution of words as simple names, short captions or more extensive complimentary texts.

In Strand's essays each image was particular to that person or place at that time but many were also universal in that they described a commonly held, identifiable humanity. What this foretold for me was that whilst each story would have its own theme, it may be that underlining all my stories was a meta-theme about the human condition, or the nature of existence, or???

This structure – working from the specific to the general, from the plain of visceral reality to universal concepts has, since then, provided me an underlying structure for forming stories. And it also taught me to ask: *"does this or that image have meaning only within the essay or does it have some other merits, to clearly reveal the human condition or whatever the meta-story is?"*

There was also something different in his photographs, something I had only sensed in other's works from earlier in the 20th century. The famous French photographer, Henri Cartier- Bresson gave voice to pre-visualizing the moment when you release the shutter. That is when the subject's action within the frame approached the most significant expressive form and at the same time approached the highest point of the action or emotion. Have a look:

FIND: henri+cartier+bresson

This consciousness of merging form and content he called the 'decisive moment' – a phrase that alerted many to the notion that there could be no randomness in the act of photographing.

The viewer then sees a singular moment in history, an action played out by an individual or a group of individuals never to be repeated.
For a moment look at Strand's pictures again.

FIND: paul+strand+landscape

There are no indications that people are about to do
something. They seem to be contented to wait for
Strand to release the shutter, which gives a different
sense to the *time* captured within the image. It is a
moment in *time* that seems to have lasted for hours
or years, or forever and that will continue to be, once
the shutter had been released.

Cartier-Bresson's images are of fleeting moments,
they show *time* as it passes – for him time is an active
verb. Strand's images are of *time* as history – for him
time is a noun, an expression of eternity. It was as
though he knew he was photographing a narrative
of history while also making history.

This touches on something else: One time I was
gazing at a Brancusi sculpture, called Bird in Space.

FIND: brancusi+sculpture+bird+in+space

To me it is a fine piece of sculpture, elegant and
thrilling, which becomes a bird in flight. But in its
reductive distillation, it becomes the essence of
Brancusi's idea of flight. It describes for me an
aesthetic perfectibility which affirms, for a brief
moment, that we humans are not only capable of
stupidity and cruelty but of immense knowledge,
love and creativity. It shows that which is essential
and reminds me of watching an ocean or a
mountain; where the 'essential' encourages a
memory of the eternal.

Strand's calm images with their solid immobile
people, their simple, unremarkable, almost plain
compositions, and the softness of his prints with
neither deep blacks not blown out whites, are also

only of what is essential and therefore they too allude to the eternal.

SEE 9: Compositions influenced by Strand

As most kids, I lived inside a narrow world but I insisted in asking 'what was there to photograph?' There must be a reason to direct my camera, a point of focus and a point of view to be chosen, consciously or not. I began to suspect that every decision had within it a meaning and importance for the final print; that the choice of shutter speed, lens length and all else would ultimately reinforce or undermine my intentions.

Strand helped me to understand what was to be allowed within the frame is vital to seeing a complete idea, and what was unnecessary had to be excluded as a distraction. I tried to reduce my images to simpler forms and lines using limited depth of focus, by framing or printing, by cropping or darkening what was inessential or distracting.

SEE 10: Storytelling influenced by Strand

Strand led me to the value of narrative storytelling whilst also leading me to think reductively not only about the picture's visual components but as well about trying not to be obvious– allowing the picture to offer and the viewer to receive without exaggerating in inappropriate ways.

CARAVAGGIO'S HUMBLE SUBJECTS

Caravaggio, the late 16th century Italian painter, was, to quote an early source, *"a hot headed murderer who overwhelmed his contemporaries while breaking the rules with huge energy, by painting"*, and as another contemporary wrote, *"with so much appetite, spice and flavour that others could only swim in his wake"*.

His work has had a direct affect upon my picture making emotionally and visually.

FIND: caravaggio+sacrifice+of+isaacs

Was Caravaggio just a flawed man? Or was he in fact a brilliant artist of the people whose extraordinary talent provided a startling view of life that most of his wealthy status craving middle class critics, who numbered amongst his many enemies, studiously attempted to ignore?

And why? Because he displayed in his work what was to others, an offensive reality of gritty life-fullness, poverty and hardship to represent Biblical saints and their trials. He moved the saints from the palaces to the streets, and in that simple act, threatened the wealthy classes ownership of saintliness.

FIND: caravaggio+incoronazione

FIND: caravaggio+madonna+and+child+with+st+anne

Look at those pictures - these are rough looking people with gnarled muscles and sun burnt skin rather than the refined puppets and dolls of other's sanitized depictions of reality as you can see here by his contemporary Bartolomeo Bassi.

FIND: bartolomeo+bassi+painter

Caravaggio democratized subject matter. He was the first to honour neither the rich nor the rising middleclass, but the underpaid workers and the urban poor by using them as his subjects.

Having come from a middleclass background, his sympathy for the poor was an early sign of how an artist who forsakes the aspirations of his own class for those of the powerless, regardless of his own income or education, becomes déclassé or 'without a class' by virtue of beliefs and a desire to show a different set of truths.

Caravaggio's painful, exquisitely lit images deeply affected my understanding of picture making. He, as the other artists, provide ways of seeing, and a visual vocabulary. His visceral depiction of humble people helped me to more clearly see the banality of celebrity culture and my own class's concerns for the signs of status and wealth.

He turned me away from being in awe of those things to becoming disdainful of a popular culture that diffuses and diminishes the reality of most people's lives.

It is also the aliveness and presence of his characters which so affected my own work.

SEE 11: Pictures influenced by Caravaggio

Many painters were then depicting an idealised romantic, religious or glorious world on behalf of their patrons as in this painting by one of Caravaggio's contemporaries, Fragonard.

FIND: fragonard+woman+on+a+swing

This candied image was hardly the reality of most people's lives. Caravaggio painted the world he lived within and witnessed. He was there; it was alive for him. Some readers may see that I'm pointing out a conflict between a fantasy of life and a rising realism, between an entertaining baroque distraction of sun tinted clouds with puffy cherubs and a clear-eyed documentation of most people's lived lives of hunger, illness and poverty.

This touches not only upon what we perceive but also upon what we make of what we see. A poet may witness life with great delicacy, a composer may hear the world of the streets but both – as all other makers of art, may recreate the world whilst in a remote loft, whilst the documentary photographer or film-maker must be in front of that world they comment on. The limited perceptions artists carry back to their studio must be nurtured with their imaginations. It is this fusion between the perceived and the imagined that makes art.

The documentarist needs to possess a sense of 'there-ness' which demands 100% presence and at the same time, the imagined creative transformation of that presence into a finished work which will only be possible if, at the time of the events, he or she has recorded sufficient information for the later editing to be able to tell the full, multi-dimensional story.

It is so often about seeing the conjunction of people, emotions and other influences that say, be ready, something is about to happen– as in these pictures of mine.

SEE 12: pictures influenced by Caravaggio's sense of immediacy

As the there-ness is an intensification of perception, for me, my presence is an intensification of living life in the moment, but a moment in which all of my knowledge, experiences, preferences, culture and education come to an unquantifiable split second in which the accumulated elements of who I am affirm 'this is the moment to say yes', to release the shutter, to record the decisive moment.

Caravaggio's paintings touched me in another way. His use of angular, out of frame single source lighting produced a struggle between illumination and darkness, between the clarity of the illuminated and mystery of the unseen, between the comprehensible and the incomprehensible, and in formal picture terms: that is to say, 'in the look of the image' he used this lighting to emphasise the drama of the story.

FIND: caravaggio+adoration+of+the+shepherds

FIND: caravaggio+le+sette+opere+di+misercordia

His light became expressive content, and as I came to think of it, light became a character in my stills and films as in these three pictures:

SEE 13: Light with character

His reduced palette of burnt sienna, ochre, muddy browns and blacks created massive areas of contrast

with the blacks always anchoring the image and its
characters in darkness, as if life-filled highlights
enter a conflict with the unidentifiable.

To sum up: Caravaggio taught me to honour the
everyman and woman; he taught me to see the
importance of light and especially the beauty and
drama of single source lighting and in particular of
window light; his limited use of colour taught me
the beauty of a reduced palette, and he made me
aware of the importance of not only being there but
being aware of being there.

W. EUGENE SMITH

The American photojournalist W. Eugene Smith
naturally follows on from Caravaggio in his use of
contrast, his implied menace of darkness, in the way
he claws highlights out of that shadows as well as in
precarious compositions that teeter on
disintegration.

Also there is something similar in their spirits-
seeing that life is a struggle, and that the poor and
humble need to continually fight against
overwhelming odds.

As I said earlier, photographers and documentary
film-makers have no choice but to be present to do
what they do. Once they have witnessed events,
spent the time of their lives, sometimes under threat,
photographing, editing, printing and delivering,
how are their pictures then selected by
commissioning editors, clients or publishers who
have not been there?

Smith was clear about this problem. He fought against his editors because he saw *"a whole world view (his) being substituted by another world view (the editor's)"*. He struggled against this editorial control his whole career.

Once I had fallen in love with his images, his troublesome rebellion fed me as if a blood transfusion. This transfusion eventually led me to be convinced that my responsibility was not to the editors and art directors who commissioned me, but to the story, to the truth, and especially to the people who allowed me into their lives.

I recognised it was my duty to the people in my images to tell their story, and to not allow the editor's or publisher's world views to distort it. Needless to say, I created a rocky road for myself as it became clear that to take the side of the poor, the oppressed or the working class was to oppose the imposition of middleclass values which are almost always in service to those who pay their salaries.

Even with having understood some of this from Caravaggio's problems in 16th century Italy, I had naively assumed that in a late 20th century democracy, it would be otherwise. Silly me. This is an eternal dilemma.

FIND: masters+of+photography+image+smith+minimata

John Berger, the English author and painter, wrote about a Sicilian painter named Antonello da Messina (1430-1479), that his work represented *"Sicily, (an) island which admits passion and refuses illusions"*.

For me, Berger's observation about the Sicilian painter is an accurate description of how Smith was and how I learned to be committed to storytelling: *'admitting passion while refusing illusion'*.

This is one of my earliest photo-stories:

SEE 14: Autism Clinic, New York City, 1968

Of course I didn't and still don't understand many truths but I'm sufficiently conscious to hold in check my own emotional distortions of what I believe to be 'the truth'. I think that the battle to grasp truth is less important that the moral and emotional determination to wish to do so.

In other words, I recognise I am less important than the story; that I am a servant and an expression of others; that my utility is to give the voiceless a voice; to expose what is hidden; to make visible what is abstract; to understand that the most important pronoun is 'we' and not 'me'.

And one thing more: that I believe in sombre times society needs artists to devote themselves to two things: to foster the ability for others to resist the endless attrition of our humanity, and to create beauty so profoundly needed to sensitize us to what humans are capable of. This is not a prescription but a plea.

I wish to create grace, tenderness, compassion, a respect for others and for the trials of life and death, and how we are a part of where we come from.

In the midst of the 1960's struggles against racism and the Vietnam War, W. Eugene Smith said about photographing on Sipan during the Pacific war in 1944 that "but for the luck of my US birth my people could be these people, my children could be those children."

FIND: w+eugene+smith+ Sipan+pictures

> *"I saw my daughter and my wife and my mother and my son reflected in the tortured faces of another race; and each time I pressed the shutter release it was a shouted condemnation, and that I hoped (the image) might survive through the years and at least echo through the minds of people who are searching for profound meaning."*

One of Smith's most famous essays is the *Pittsburgh Story*, which is dark, brooding and filled with people animated by stress and loss, and by cityscapes tempered by fire and choked by smoke.

FIND: w+eugene+smith+pittsburgh+essay

Smith, more than all others, taught me that in capturing precious moments in the lives of others, through my presence, and spending the time of my life thinking about, traveling to and taking the time to photograph, and then processing, editing and printing an image, I too may pay a debt of responsibility to others and I too may find some redemption in what is otherwise a world which drives us to unacceptable compromises; a world in which not only our actions, but our inactions injure others.

For a moment I want to contrast Smith with Paul Strand. The difference is not just in the subject matter, but in the way in which the two men understood the world around them.

Strand, the well-read left wing intellectual, lived in a luminous world of rationality, in which all people had dignity and purpose.

Smith, the war-torn photojournalist, saw a hellish world of self-destructive madness in which he sought redemption as he carved his subjects out of worrying shadows.

Smith's editorial struggles are echoed in the conflict of shadows and highlights within his photographs, and in his ability to capture precise moments of frailty, exhaustion, defeat, confusion and madness in his stories.

More than anyone else, to me, Smith's work combined Da Vinci's humanity, Weston's life of art, Michelangelo's struggle for freedom, Strand's aspiration for intellectual clarity and the eternal, and Caravaggio's rebellion against the dominant but false values of his day and his use of light as a character commenting on reality.

All of those artists consummated in Smith's work and led me to aspire to a kind of humane poetry in my own pictures, and while making photographs and films, at some point I recognised that I too was attempting to give shape and meaning to existence, as in these:

SEE 15: Giving shape and meaning

And now, a contemporary artist...

RICKY ROMAIN

Ricky Romain, an English painter, whose body of work is dedicated to human rights. Ricky has become a friend, not because I seek friends or friendship but because when I saw his work I realised that his concerns and mine were and are very similar. I saw details in his paintings were like those I have long sought through my lenses and feel empathy for, and have been convinced they are redolent with what it means to be human.

SEE 16: Ricky Romain's paintings and Robert Golden's photographs

Ricky is concerned with feelings rather than the current preoccupation of 'things'. His feelings possess him as he offers them with tenderness in his images. He uses the language of action- to paint- to relieve him of the oppressive burden.

SEE 17: Ricky painting

The modest things that count to him in his day-by-day life are tools and vital materials: canvas, gesso, brushes, pencils, oils, turpentine, charcoal and oil sticks. Also his richly illustrated notebooks filled with swathes of colour lead to his more austere finished canvases.

SEE 18: Ricky Romain's painting details and notebooks

They lead in two ways. The first is by working through emotions, characters, ideas and perhaps a trope of colour or lines that may be recognised only as minor diversions not weighty enough to be exported to his large canvases. And then there are forms that whisper they are of substance, ready to stand amongst the other visitors who occupy his canvases.

They shadow him, a dark form that he momentarily embraces as he 'attacks the canvas' in a fury of actions tracing his emotions in marks, rubbings and scrapings until finally, the disappeared- lost lovers, parents and children re-appear but as memories transformed each and every one into a commemoration– dignified, but trapped in paint, saddened for all of us.

SEE 19: series of Ricky Romain's paintings and details

Ricky is self-conscious. For some this leads to self-preoccupation. For some, as Ricky, it is a curse imposed upon those who are susceptible to other's agony. Because of this, he conjures his character's beings out of an imagination nurtured by compassion, and out of the inexplicable madness of others. Often he asks, "Why", as should we all.

His paintings address the human condition stranded between existing and an un-resolved end.

SEE 20: The human condition

Look at them, they are also particular in the way a person is stalked by a chimera; the way a spirit observes our human frailty, the way one person supports another, or the way one person aligns his memories and another bends his head clasping his losses to himself, and a man, who could be Willy Loman from Arthur Miller's *Death Of A Salesman*, holds his son who holds Willy's guilt.

SEE 21: Trapped within impending tragedy

These are moments of impending tragedy. People trapped, awaiting a passport, a ticket to freedom, a bureaucrat's or judge's decision.

You can hear Mengele saying *"left"* to her (she will die), *"right"* to him, (he will live), you can hear the apparatchik saying *"historical necessity deems you must sacrifice your children for the cause"*, you can hear the politicians braying, *"this is a just war, sacrifice your flowers of youth"*.

For all of human history this has been a universal condition but for each individual it is a particular situation. When not just looked at but seen closely; they are like discovering images of a documentary photographer. They are both still and yet filled with energy that vibrates within each character as they await their fate.

I think these photographs of mine have some of those qualities I see in Ricky's paintings:

SEE 22: Robert Golden's stills related to Ricky Romain's painting

We, the viewers, stand outside of their plight, perhaps gaping as visitors to a concentration camp, perhaps wondering why we too seem transfixed.

It is because Pol Pot, Pinochet, Milosevic, and Mussolini, Hitler, Stalin, and now Trump and Kim Jong Un echo in our memories.

"We are not safe", announce the characters in Ricky's paintings and perhaps in some of my pictures. These paintings are uncomfortable. What else could they be? Ricky continues to inquire, to persecute himself and to pester his art with unquiet questions at twice the age when most people surrender to the conventional ideas that surround all of us. Perhaps he could have been a writer or a scientist but for our good fortune he is a painter.

With all of the angst within each frame, they are also a love song to the innocent, the gentle, and the kind hearted lover or parent, to the trusting child we all care for, and an invocation for us to remember that before we are white or black, red or brown, before we are Christian, Moslem or Jew, before we are straight or gay, bright or dull, we are human.

SEE 23: Affection

This is metaphysics (a philosophy of being) rather than description. Ricky's paintings evoke pain in our psyche because they challenge who we are and what we allow or what we turn away from. In this way, this artist provides for us what art offers: a reminder of our humanity, a balm of truth, a glimmer of reason and hope and yes that inexplicable fragrance of love and beauty. These are some of the things I have been given by pictures.

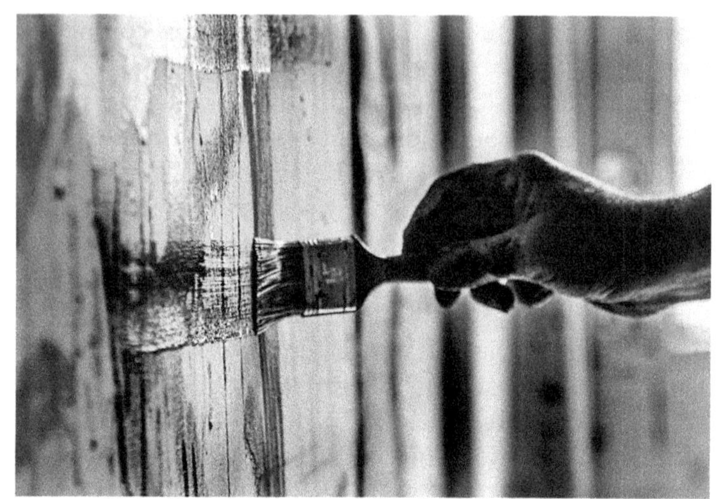

Ricky Romain painting, 2015; photo Robert Golden

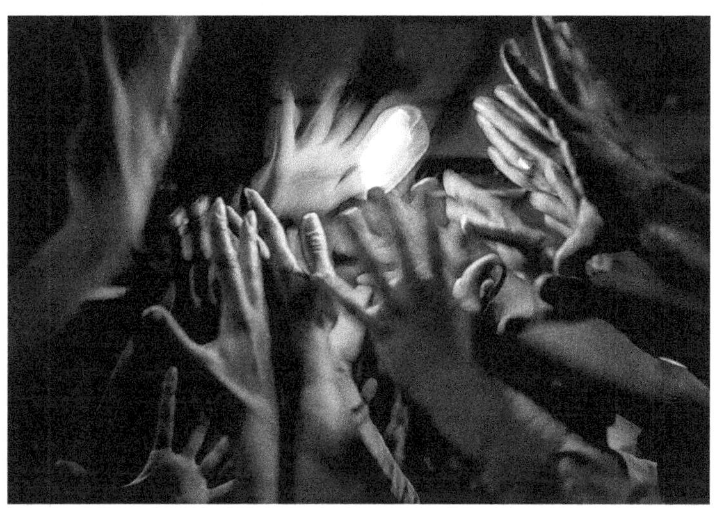

The Light, from The Complete Freedom of Truth project,
Bournemouth University, Aug 16; photograph: Robert Golden

2
PROCESS
CURIOSITY FIRST

Making films or photographs, as any creative form, begins with curiosity and with an itch. Without curiosity you have no need nor desire to enter what is often a time consuming exercise. Without the itch, an inexplicable desire to take the ever moving, ever changing and unpredictable three-dimensional flesh and blood world, and to coax the light reflecting from it through a lens, transforming it into a frozen two-dimensional artefact, which is a representation rather than actual life. Without that itch, this task is too arduous to pursue.

This curiosity is the same a child has when she asks, *'what is this'* and *'what is that?'* It is not a 'childish' act but filled with the innocence of 'child-like' curiosity, of trying to make sense of her world.

For me, I must keep asking 'why' until there is no other 'why' left. Given my knowledge and personality at that moment in my life I will have reached as far down into the essence of the thing as I can, although perhaps five years later I will revisit the same thought, concern or film and understand it differently. That is why each generation needs to revisit the classics. This process is like adding ingredients to a sauce, then cooking them down until only the syrup is left and beyond that it burns into bitterness.

There are two essential curiosities: the first is of the outer world with its wild, unknown, dangerous and

tantalizing hills and valleys beyond our own
horizons.

The second curiosity, surrounded by one's own
exterior life, often restricted in its freedom and social
mobility, is the inner life of the psyche. There we can
discover unlimited dreams and desires. There, as a
reaction to our embrace of the surrounding world,
we may discover creativity.

Together these two spheres of activity describe a
whole reality, a fusion between the inner and outer
dimensions of our lives. Both are real and valid, both
hold adventures for the soul and the mind, both can
be investigated through one's creative work.

Beyond these curiosities there is something else: the
imaginings of an essence. Without being able to
imagine, or more specifically, to pre-visualize the
possible existence of a thing, we cannot make it. We
do not know what to make, how to construct it and
out of what techniques and materials.

First off we must be able to imagine the things
essence, that it can be something, that it can be
conjured into life starting with our recognition of
its possible existence and ending with the thing
(photograph, novel, song) itself.

The only thing that pre-exists this is the individual
human being's existence within a society. If you
recognise this, you also must recognise that all
cultural production is based on the being of an
individual in a society of others, which is at a certain
level of technical, scientific development – the

development that offers the tools and materials for creating the imagined thing.

This may seem like an unnecessary abstraction but it helps to appreciate the point that no art nor story retold nor report is anything other than a subjective response to the surrounding world, something which confronts the notion of objectivity; especially when the so-called objectivity is used as an authoritative decision making device to rule over the rest of us.

PERMANENT QUESTIONING

All artists need to be in a state of permanent questioning and curiosity. Sven Lindqvist, the Swedish writer asked:

> *"Is it the function of art to make mass graves banal? Is it the task of thought to make starvation uninteresting? Spiritual happiness that makes the world irrelevant will also make suffering, oppression and extermination irrelevant."*

It is not just the social/political world that I am concerned with but also the inescapable human and personal questions of love, beauty and death, the ever present: 'why are we here' and 'how can we contribute'? These questions are a part of what one has to say and a part of what one can use the arts for.

Our confusion, uncertainty, self-doubt as well as our loves and hates are human responses we all relate to. The more truthfully and clearly we represent even the negative attitudes, the more the rest of us will gain from those creative struggles.

The best of one's private world, expressed eloquently, can heal wounds and provide people a sense of solidarity with others whom one does not know but shares pain and pleasure with. The work serves as a bridge which crosses time, cultures, language and class barriers and which overcomes existential loneliness. This is where a teenager says, *"I get this, that writer is talking to me"*.

THE ROLE OF IDEOLOGY

Most people admit to believing in a set of values or, more mystically, in an energy, often described as 'a life force' or a god. Both admit, consciously or not, to the acceptance of a set of beliefs. A set of beliefs is reasonably called an ideology (a creed, a dogma). It is simply a part of one's understanding of existence.

Perhaps the word 'ideology' seems a bit serious or grand but in fact it is fair to apply it to any set of beliefs about how we conduct our lives, however incoherent. Maybe that is the problem: that many people do not have a coherent set of beliefs and are happy enough to live in a kind of fog of opinions, half understood realities, wishes and hopes.

Every coherent and incoherent set of beliefs, that is to say, every ideology should not be thought of as a mirror of truth, but rather a refracted view of truth. Each ideology will probably include vague hopes expressing a dream or nightmarish model of reality, or it may be a cynical or optimistic view. Whatever it is, it is not reality itself. This distinction is key to people being able to understand that there are competitive and contradictory belief systems or ideologies held by others that will also refract a subjective view of truth.

Culture (the sum total of all we think and make), and in particular art, is a refraction of our beliefs – it is a kind of reality filtered by our imaginations and our specific ideology. Ideology is necessary in that it allows people to place themselves in a world they imagine exists. It helps people negotiate what they imagine reality to be, allowing them to fit in and to cope. It provides a worldview and indicates the ethical boundaries they choose to live within.

Ideologies are mostly based on un-measurable subjective constructions – a set of beliefs connected in various rational and irrational ways to each other, which we inherit from educational institutions, family, popular culture and common knowledge.

All cultural production and therefore all art is the result of an inherited worldview; therefore each cultural production is the result of a particular ideology whether we have examined it or not.

All films, photographs, songs, poems, novels, music we make within our particular ideological refraction are an allusion (a hint, an insinuation, an oblique reference) to truth rather than truth itself.

Another way to say this is that there is a chasm between our constructed ideology with which we think we comprehend reality and our misapprehension of that reality because those views are wrapped in a muddle of religious cant, superficial popular culture assumptions, poor educational practice and government and corporate propaganda.

The chasm between these two states exists within and between individuals as well as between dominant and subjugated classes. People with wealth have a profoundly different view of their right to wealth, power, justice, freedom and democracy than those without wealth.

The Guardian Newspaper recently pointed out that the average charity donation per year of British people possessing over 10 million pounds is £240. Their every murmur and all culture they commission or purchase is an expression, not of charity but of their ideological beliefs and tastes just as are the rest of ours. They do not allow news to be published or broadcast that is contradictory to their belief system, as they will not purchase a painting or finance a film or commission an article that will admit to another reality. The ruling elite wants to maintain the status quo through imposing one view - theirs on the rest of us. This does not make a society of plural thinking and discussion; that is, it does not make a demos-kratos (ancient Greek for the people's voice or power) society, one that holds to itself the need for the voice of the people to make it valid and alive with debate. It makes for a hierarchical semi-totalitarian society expressing one voice – that of the rulers.

How do we engage our ideas and attitudes to make art that satisfies our needs and our community's needs? We cannot generalize in that each artist brings to bear his or her history, culture, understanding, prejudices, injuries, fears, hopes, skills and talent within a specific community at a specific moment in history. We cannot generalize.

As I have written in the other essays, artists need to understand their relation to power and wealth. In the most minimal way they need answer the question for themselves – *"do I acquiesce to, or accept the status quo as a reasonable and humane state of being or not"*?

If so, then the person hoping to be an artist will be serving those who create oppression and manufacture quiescence. The aspiring artist will be on the wrong side of history, the side that relegates them to become decorators, entertainers and tools of the dominant ideology accepting their rulers/bosses/owners narrow cultural canon. In this position the artist's commissioner/sponsor/ editor may support liberal causes – as gender or limited racial and religious equality, but they will always reject artists if they question the structures of wealth and power.

To accept being on the outside of the artistic or commercial marketplace is difficult. Every potential artist must find a way to survive emotionally, intellectually and financially whilst making art that is relevant to their community and their age. In the present Anglo-Saxon world it is unlikely they will do anything of real value in the struggle for justice and freedom if they work inside the cultural canon.

I have worked for many years producing hundreds of photo-essays, commercials, advertisements, magazine articles, book and record covers and a number of illustrated books. In all that time, with all of that work, whilst I have made a living, I do not think more than 2 or 3 projects have had any humane value. Only the work I have financed myself by doing that commercial work has had any social worth.

In this double life I came to understand several things. First I accepted that in an immoral world – the world owned and operated by the .01%, it is not possible to live a moral life.

Second, that many people I encountered in my professional life, although mostly unconscious of what they were doing, acted as gatekeepers to the barbican ruled by their managers/creative directors/gallery owners/editors/or publishers highly defended anti-humane ideology.

Third, both of these things meant I had to accept my day job was contradictory to my morality and ethics, but I also had to accept my guilt was a reality. I refused to fool myself into thinking that what I did was right or good. From my encounters with others, it seems that many bright and talented people preferred to believe the life they led was whole and correct, thus they repressed their better instincts to lead a life of contradiction and anxiety.

STORY TELLING

We need stories to understand who and what we are
and where we our on our journey. We need stories
to discover empathy for others and to occasionally
escape reality. Stories help us to become more
complete by challenging our fragmented and
alienating world.

A story can be defined as a succession of related
events structured with a beginning, middle and an
end. Stories differ from history, which is also a
succession of related events, although different in
that a story is a product of imagination and a history
retells what is considered to be factual research.

Ben Okri, the African writer, wrote, *"stories are like
rivers that take us into unknown lands, or like travellers
that take us into forgotten dreams."* Artists and
students need to regard this, as both need to offer
hope and possibilities through telling well told tales.

Through separating the practice of storytelling into
form, content and technique I help people to
understand that the point of making is to discover
what is real and truthful to them and then to be
sincere with it as they devise ways to communicate
with an audience whom they wish their work to
embrace.

When a photograph or film pictures something
humane, kind or generous, this is more than an act
of rebellion, it is a reminder that in the face of all the
deceits, misinformation and lies which surround us

day by day, it is possible that we can hang on to our humanity.

This is why I am committed to storytelling with pictures.

FOUR PRACTICES

The following is a guide I use with people I teach. It may not be for everyone, but it can lead to interesting discoveries. I am making a few assumptions: that artists want to create work that speaks to others; that work which speaks to others can only do so if it addresses people's needs and wants; and finally that often neither the natural audience nor the artist is aware of those needs or wants, or if so, they have not figured out what gives rise to them.

This method helps artists to connect what concerns them in the middle of the night with making photographs (films, literature, fine arts) that connect with the concerns of a community. This is a process of recognizing themes.

The first stage of this is to experiment with mind mapping.

SUBJECT MATTER AND CONTENT

Before I explain mind-mapping I will separate the concepts of subject matter, content and theme.

The surface of reality, the things, people and places you photograph are the Subjects within the frame but they constitute neither the theme nor the content, both of which lie behind/within such subjects as flowers, dancers, miners. For the ease of discussion, theme is the unifying idea from picture to picture and perhaps essay to essay - for instance, a concern about the uses of political power or the suffering of the elderly. Content is the structure that holds or enwraps the theme. Your theme may be about political power, your content would be a story that can reveal the nature of that power, for instance, the anti-democratic nature of arbitrary politicians and the subject of the photographs would be the people and places of a particular political party.

As an example of the differences between subject matter and content: I grew up with a dislike of bullies. This informed my emotional responses to many things about politics. In fraught situations I would seek ways to show the humanity of the underdog. I have an instinctual empathy for the impoverished, the weak and victims of the strong and powerful. Across the years this has formed a visible emotional undercurrent, and a dominant theme in my work. The theme of injustice gives rise to revealing the content, for instance, inequality.

The difficult part is always recognising and gaining access to people and places – subject matter - that may manifest your theme and content. Once you have the chosen subject matter and your underlying content is bubbling away on a more or less conscious level, there are always sets of questions about what is honest, correct, morally acceptable and indeed, what is the truth in front of us.

Many years ago I read about a then well known British journalist named James Cameron. During the Korean War, just after he first arrived in a combat zone, he was soon writing his highly regarded dispatches. Another journalist, who had been there for several months previous to Cameron's arrival, asked him how he managed to so quickly figure out what was happening in the confused situation. Cameron responded that he relied upon his own ethics to understand what was right and what was wrong.

The challenge in life for us all is to make sense of our existence. Making pictures has always helped me to make sense and to create some meaning out of living.

I recently made a film about Monika Pagneux, one of Europe's great movement directors for theatre. It is a name that people in the profession know but as she is a *behind-the-curtain* person, she is not a name recognized by the general public. At 86 she is a master filled with knowledge of her profession, which is to help actors prepare for the stage, but she is much more. She knows that it is necessary for the actors to not 'represent' but 'to be'. She had taught the necessity of finding ways to discover the truth in every scene and character. Monika's inspirational way of working allows actors to find a flow or unity between their inner psyche and its outer expression. Truth becomes the source of creativity; actions are a result of being, not thinking.

This describes a kind of grace, one that I aspire to. Searching for the truth is difficult but wishing to do so should not be. If we find some grace in the search, I believe part of it rests in our decision to confront our demons and to decide the search itself is vital to creativity.

What is clear to me is that the same underlying passions inform how I make a landscape as well as how I make a still life, a portrait or how I approach a street battle or moments in a theatre rehearsal. The common element is me, my belief system, my emotional response to life. I am not a mirror; I am a very particular prism, as are we all.

PRACTICE

Mind Mapping for Content

I suspect many know about this practice.

Get an easy to use pen, pencil or marker and a large clean, unlined piece of paper … do not do this on a computer.

Find time when you can spend several hours on your own without pressure, demands or other people's presence. You need concentration, quiet and privacy to do this successfully.

These three things - concentration, quiet and privacy – can be intimidating to some people because a space is left in which one must face one's self. Unless you are already 100% committed to some content you know and care about, and even if so, you will find this process revealing.

Begin to write down, randomly on the paper,
individual words that stand for
•ideas/concepts/conditions,
•individuals/groups of individuals
•emotions
that presently concern you, that spring to mind in
the middle of the night. In all three categories write
both positive and negative examples.

Ideas/Concepts/Conditions may be 'liberalism',
'aesthetics', 'religion', 'nationalism', 'intellectualism',
'illness' and so on. It is best to stick to
ideas/concepts/conditions that play a real part in
your life rather than completely abstract ideas. If, for
instance, you are concerned about other people's
poverty, the state of democracy or social fairness,
write those things down. Or if you question the
meaning of beauty or of life, write those things
down.

Individuals/Groups may be 'father', 'boy friend',
'lover', 'grandma', or 'politicians', 'monks', 'writers',
a religious sect, a corporation or government agency,
etc.

Emotions may be, 'envy', 'love', avarice or contempt,
etc.

Do not construct a list – write them any and
everywhere on the paper. As you continue, fewer
words will come to mind. Stop when you begin
splitting hairs or repeating yourself. There will only
be so many concerns at any one time in your life.

Once you have finished, look at the page and think
about what you have written. Ask yourself if this is a
fair appraisal of the things that concern you. If
others pop up, write them down. Think again,
appraise again and when you are satisfied that you
have emptied yourself of these concerns, begin to
connect them by drawing circles around them and a
line between the circled concerns. It is possible that
one circle may be connected to several other circles.
For instance, the name of a person may be connected
to 'love', to another person and to 'loneliness'.

It is important to be certain that real links are made.
Of course, all things in our lives are connected
because our being and consciousness connects them,
but try to limit the connections to those that seem to
be important links.

Okay, perhaps a bit threatening or worrying so far
but fairly simple to do. Now study the clusters of
circles you have made. This is where it gets a bit
more challenging. Try to provide each cluster with a
very short title. You may have connected 'dad' with
'illness'. You might call this 'Fear For Dad'. Or
maybe you have connected your child's name with
'school fees' with 'success' and you might name that
'Children's Education'.

Once you have done this, take another sheet of
paper and list the cluster names in order of
importance to you. Have a thought. These are the
things that are, at that moment, central to your life,
your concerns, your loves and preoccupations.
These may offer you real content to consider.

Deciding On Subject Matter

Take the top three titles from Practice 1 and ask yourself what they really mean to you. For instance, lets say your top concern is 'Fear for Dad'. Perhaps this indicates your dependency on his wisdom, your unqualified love for him or your relief that he may soon drop off his perch? You need to think this through and be as honest as possible with yourself. You also need to ask yourself if you have the resilience to confront him and yourself about your perceived truths.

If Dad agrees to be photographed, you have your subject matter but only as a form of unshaped clay. Photographing dad is vague and it is not possible to make pictures of vague subject matter.

Let us say, for the sake of an example, most of your responses add up to describe love. That may mean it is time to celebrate his life so far, to ask all the things you wanted to, to spend an hour with him once a day or once a week photographing him and if not him, the things around him.

What does he have in his pockets?
What does his closet look like?
What chair does he sit in?
What foods or drinks does he consume?

You may decide to describe him with a series of relevant landscapes and/or still life images. Perhaps you photograph all of his family and friends – of the human world around him that constitutes his society.

If he will let you photograph him, perhaps do a portrait each day or list 10 activities of his and photograph him involved in those from eating breakfast to reading the paper.

But I have got ahead of myself in terms of story telling. I simply want you to see how this process works to lead you to real content (love of one's father), and to subject matter photographed as landscapes, still-life, portraits or documentary images.

This practice will have taken you from your chosen content to a particular subject matter that is a metaphor or an example of the content and it may have indicated to you how it should be photographed.

Before you return to the following practice see the website of photographer Phillip Toledano, a man I do not know but you can view how something so close and familiar can become a work of profound emotional truth:

FIND: Phillip+Toledano +days+with+my+father

See an essay: "I AM STILL ME, by Joy Unglo, a woman I taught. *https://www.robertgoldenpictures.com/people-robert-taught/*

Finding The High Concept
Let's say you develop a passion to photograph the inner lives of eight year olds. Your Subjects naturally become eight-year-old children.
Immediately you will ask 'which children?' Do you choose only children of a particular class, race,

gender, religion or other predisposition? If so, why have you made those choices?

Although the children are the Subjects, these primary choices call to question what your Theme and Content is. What do you think you are doing, investigating and revealing? What is your interest in this proposal? What compels you to pursue this? What does it say about you? Is this, for instance, your inner lost child seeking an answer to lifelong questions? Are you imposing your predispositions, religious or secular beliefs on a set of assumed facts without being truthful, without really questioning? Do you believe there is a universal discussion within your choices or is it, in your view, pedestrian?

This clearly becomes an issue when you consider that if you are exposing at say $1/100^{th}$ of a second, every second you have a hundred fragments you can possibly shoot. As you become more visually literate you will begin to ask 'why shoot then rather than now?' That will be answered as greater clarity develops in what you are wishing to say, in knowing that behind every shot are sets of conscious and unconscious assumptions. Are you searching for wonder, joy, fear? Are you somehow predisposed to disregard happiness for sadness or vice versa because of your own assumptions?

I believe that this kind of enquiry can be confusing and can lead to inaction for some, but for many it will lead to deeper and richer levels of self-knowledge, a clearer interaction with the world and a more refined creativity.

Once you have recognized the content or theme that interests you, once you have chosen the subject matter, and when you have decided how to photograph it, you will need to decide how to deliver the content via an exhibition, an album, a book, on-line etc.

This set of tasks establishes a vision about communicating what you think, feel and care about to others via your photographs.

To clarify your ideas, an excellent exercise is to write a one-page explanation of your project as if you are going to explain it to others. This one-pager is the creation of private notes, not a literary masterpiece. It is one thing to say that something is mysterious but it should not be a mystery to you.

All creative work is a process of discovery; nonetheless one needs a starting point, a sense of direction and a general idea of what you are searching for and how you will deliver it to others.

Once you have the one page, reduce it to one paragraph of no more than 100 words. This will force you to be very exact in your thinking. Suddenly you will be shedding the adverbs and adjectives and all the secondary ideas. It will demand great clarity. The important ideas will begin to stand out. The thinking you do to get the page to the paragraph may lead you to re-write the page. The process demands clarity - adopt, adapt and change.

Finally, when you are satisfied with the one paragraph, reduce it to one sentence. This becomes what is called 'the High Concept' for the project. It gives you a simple way to let people know what you are doing; it truly clarifies your project to you and provides a lasting guide for you to check the progress of your project.

If you discover that the actual making of the images, the encounter with the subjects and other outside experiences change your underlying view, it's good to make that conscious, to be honest with yourself and to re-examine your original high concept. This will help you to review your emotional, intellectual and creative patterns. This becomes an investment in this and all future projects.

There is one last notion to consider called the 'Holon'. In science and in particular, in computer science it is a bit complicated, but within creative work it can be thought of more simply. At the same time, a holon is a self contained part of a work and a complete representative of it. What this means is that every work will have within it one irreducible element (idea, theme, meaning) that is central to the work itself.

Once everything is stripped out of the meaning and content of the work, the last element standing, the one that cannot be taken without losing the essence of the work is the holon.

For instance, in the above example of the essay on children, you may strip out religious notions, affection for children, questions of race or class and find that the essay still holds together because the central idea, the holon seems to be a profound love of the innocence they represent. But hold on, is it? You may find that still that can be stripped away to discover a longing for the innocence because it alludes to your need to believe that humanity can discover a perfectibility that offers hope.

The unknown holon was, to begin with, the longing for hope in a bitter world.

Reducing the high concept to the holon allows one to more clearly see what one's aims actually are, and therefore allows an artist to create more intellectually and emotionally refined work. David Glass, an astoundingly talented writer and theatre director introduced me to this notion in his following description of my first novel:

My dear friend,
Your novel is no more a thriller than True
Detective is a police procedural. I think the
holon of your book is the story of a man's search
for meaning in the face of an apparently
meaningless and indifferent world. Like Dorothy
in the Wizard Of Oz, David leaves his
meaningless home only to find yet more
meaninglessness in the outside world. It is in a
way a tragic comedy with few laughs. He begins
his journey as a forgettable man and ends his
journey forgotten on a boat adrift in the world.
So no change. No change means it's darkly
comic. His redemption is only that he does not
forget someone else, Kate. In the last sentence
there is hope. If he has not forgotten her then he,

also might not be forgotten. So there is change.
A tragedy. Change, no change. A tragic comedy.

Discovering Form: Two experiments

One
Select 10 of your favourite photographs from the
past and place them, as prints, in front of you or, if
necessary, on a computer screen. If you do not have
a collection of pictures, choose ten pictures you like
from magazines or from on-line sources and try to
lay them out or show them on your screen all
together.

Review the ten you have selected. Set aside those
that do not immediately speak to you. Once you
have done this with as much of your library you
want to review, lay the pictures out together and
allow them to stay there for several days. Move
them into any order that calls out to you; begin to
select down the batch by removing anything that
does not seem to fit, to be a part of the whole. Do not
over intellectualize but rely on gut responses.

You may find that you have a selection left that has
an emerging theme, whether it is an
autobiographical sketch, a portrait of a loved one, a
series of your travels, or a more social story as the
building of a local school or a reportage of your
town.

Serious photography, or rather taking your
engagement with the medium seriously is different
than being a snap-shooter or a professional.

Those of you with your own photographs, I would like you to answer the questions below as simply, carefully and as truthfully as possible. There is no one to judge you. Try to uncover what you really feel. Try not to defend what you have done but look at the images clearly and do the following.

First name the subject matter as if you were looking at another person's pictures.

In other words, it is not your sister 'Milly on mom's swing ' but rather 'a girl on a swing'. It is not 'my holiday in Paris' but rather 'a young man in front of the Eiffel Tower' and so on. Do this for all the pictures.

Questions:
Subject Matter
Do you only photograph your own personal experiences - as friends and family or do you photograph other people and things that are not a part of your immediate personal life?
• Do other people's lives and other places and events interest you? Do you think they have meaning or relevance to your life?
• If you only photograph things familiar to you, are they always when people are enjoying celebrations and informal gatherings or do you ever document more intimate moments? I am not referring to sex but rather adults with their children, siblings together, your ill auntie and so on?

Light
Now look at the light in the picture.

•Were you aware of its direction, its various colours, its ability to illuminate the person or thing you were concentrating on?
•Do you think there is any beauty in the light?
•Is the light in the frame balanced - meaning that it is neither too bright - burning all the highlights in an area into white - or that light is so absent that essential detail is lost in dark shadows?

Colour
What is the colour like in your pictures?
•Is it realistic or does it appear strange – too blue, green, orange or red?
•Is it garish or subtle; soft or hard?
•Does the colour matter?
What if the colours were muted or transformed into monochrome?
•Would the picture be more or less informative or more or less better to look at?

Composition
In general, where do you place the subject in the frame?
•At the centre or not; is it high or low?
•Is the horizon straight or do you tilt the camera, consciously or not?
•If you ignore the people and things and imagine you are looking at a sphere for a head, a set of tubes for the trunk, arms and legs and so on, in other words, think of the photograph as a set of volumetric graphic forms rather than as a story, how important is the main form in relation to the others?
•Is your eye drawn to that important form and if not, why do you think that is?

• How do the strong colours and relative brightness of the colours lead you towards or away from the important subject?

•How does the relative sharpness or softness (out of focus) lead your eye towards or away from seeing the subject?

•How does the relative size of the important subject help or hinder your ability to appreciate what you thought was important?

Framing

How close or far away do you frame your pictures?

•Do you ever do a single close-up of a face or body part, or of what people's hands are doing?

•Do you ever shoot big close-ups (meaning the outline of an object is beyond the edge of the frame, so if shooting a plate of food, you would be so close that the edge of the plate is not seen)?

•Do you ever shoot a wide shot so that the people or objects are clearly seen in the context of the place they are occupying?

Clarity - focus

Is the essential subject you were concentrating on clear, in focus and sharp?

•If not, was it in movement, were you in movement, did you shake the camera, was the light very dim?

•If you used flash, were you further than 20 feet (6 metres) from them?

The Decisive Moment

When you released the shutter had you watched and waited for a particular moment as when the candles on the cake were about to be blown out, or do you tend to lift, frame and shoot?

Don't worry that you may not, at this moment, be able to articulate why or why not you do something - that will come. I am coaching you to gain an objective view of your pictures in a way that is more analytical than you are used to…and also it is a bit of a tease. I'm suggesting what you are going to encounter more.

Two
This should be done by those who have their own pictures (as above) and by those who do not have a private picture gallery of their own. Choose 10 photographic images from magazines or from on-line sources that appeal to you.

In the above practice, people who have photographs to view were, to a degree, limited, amongst other things, to their experiences and the world around them to which they had access. After all, we have only what crosses in front of our lives to photograph.

But in this choice of ten images, the world is open to you with a variety of places, people, events and experiences to choose from. Again, be patient, concentrate and try to be honest in answering the following.

Please name the categories that the images naturally fall into:
fashion
beauty
still-life
food and drink
portraits

family
news
sports
landscape
documentary
and any others you may need to invent

Did you choose your ten pictures from a variety or categories or from one or a limited number? Ask yourself why you were attracted to these categories or was it a matter of convenience? If so, should you search again before moving on?

Look at the illumination.
• Is it full of darks and lights or is it fairly soft in its passage from the darkest to the lightest in the frame?
• Is there a tendency towards liking images that gravitate towards darkness (low key) or towards lightness (high key)?

Does the illumination - the source of light - figure strongly in the images? For instance, a picture of a sun setting across a landscape is about the sun and its effects on the atmosphere, or a person sitting in a room illuminated by light entering the window is about the window light.
• Is that illumination vital to the photograph or could it have been different without changing the emotional sense of the image?

Are the images in colour or monochrome (black and white)?
• If in colour, try to describe the palette. Is it warm or cold? Is it intense, gaudy, harsh, soft, pastel?

• Does it tend towards being multi-coloured or
mono-coloured?
• Ask yourself if there are any tendencies in these
choices. For instance, you may lean towards high
contrast images in black and white or you may tend
towards a combination of black and white and
monochromatic colour or a reduced range of
colours.
• Of the colours in the images, is their a tendency
towards warm (reds, orange, yellow) or cold (green,
blue) colours?

These choices tend not to be that conscious in most
people who have not thought a lot about the world
in visual terms. They do begin to tell you what kinds
of choices you naturally and unconsciously make.
As you develop there is no harm in beginning to
follow your instincts but there is also interest in
working against them to see what you learn and
how that may enlarge your visual vocabulary.

Are the images filled with many complicated forms,
patterns, things and colours or are they simple in
composition?

Think of an image of many leaves on the ground,
then of a headshot of a person against a contrasting
background. The first is filled with many forms and
details; the later is composed of a solid form carved
out of a plain space. The former tends to be more
decorative and relies less on the structure. This is the
formal architecture of the image. It is the difference
between designing a Victorian house and a modern
house.

Is there any sense that time has been stopped and captured by the release of the shutter?

Of course every photograph is a slice of time but do the photographs make a point of this? Often sports or news images are a dramatic rendering of an important moment in the game.

Do the pictures go beyond entertainment?
•Do they touch your heart?
•Is there anything about them that you will remember?

Now that you have had this dialogue with yourself, write a few notes or synopsis from each of the above points as: *"My preference is still-life in soft light, strongly moulded by the light, in colour, which is cool pastel and simply designed in a timeless place that is somehow mysterious."* This is a way to get started, to think about what you are drawn to and to what you may want to think about photographing and in what way. Perhaps, having done this, you may want to repeat it with your new knowledge. Indeed, do it as many times as it works for you.

You may now say, *"Okay that was that choice but I do like portraits so I'll look for a variety of them and do the same to discover my taste and choices."*

IN CONCLUSION

Above are ways to approach thinking about making pictures. It is only the beginning of the journey. Amongst the many things you may encounter are:
•how to transform a theme into content (recognizing the inner emotional truths which give rise to the theme and the external manifestations that reveal the theme)
•how to select subject matter which tells the story of and reveals your chosen theme
(creating the high concept)
•how to photograph the subject matter
(what 'look' or style would be appropriate, evocative and involving? This is the beginning of a poetic vision)
•how to move from description to evocation in your picture making
(the difference between fact and emotion)
•how to make sense out of technique
(what choices do you make to create a picture which feels in its look as the right appearance for the particular theme and subject?)
•recognising the importance of storytelling
•how to discover the importance of your communications using photographs
(fine arts, literature – the role of the artist in society, social responsibility, the difference between maintaining and challenging the status quo)
•how to pre-visualize individual pictures and complete stories (storyboarding, rhythms, use of texts, captions, other media)
•how to see rather than just look … amongst many other things. Enjoy the journey.

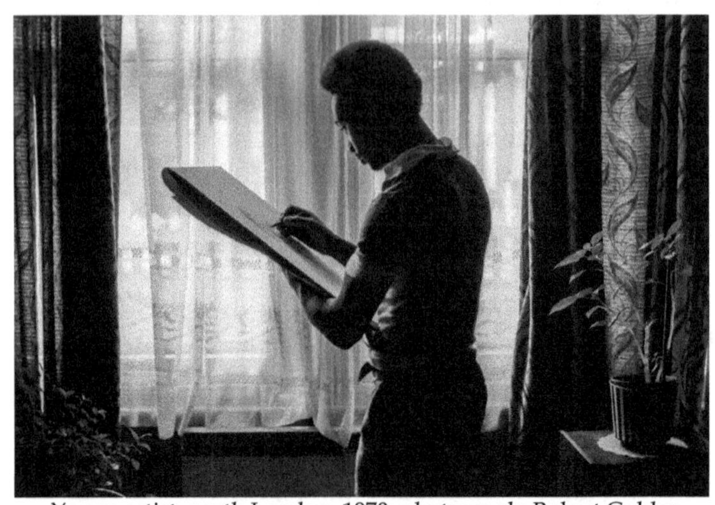

Young artist, north London, 1978; photograph: Robert Golden

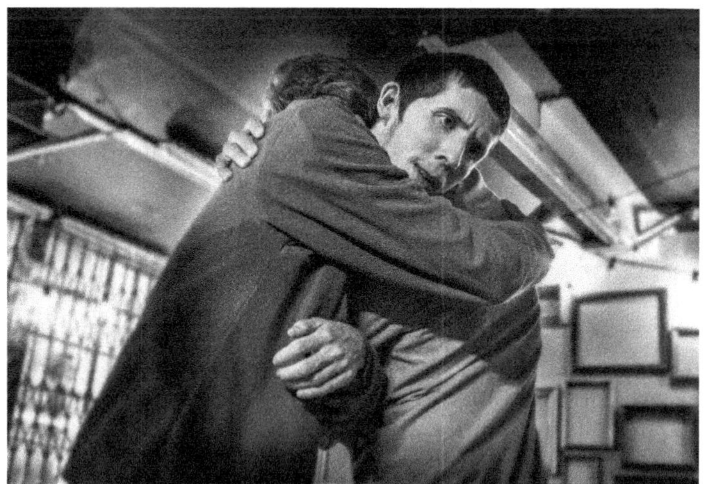

Embrace, Croydon during a Complete Freedom of Truth project,
August 2017; photograph: Robert Golden

3
UNDERLYING ASSUMPTIONS

Following are a few assumptions and definitions I use for myself that may help others to digest the above thoughts.

ART

is a particular and delicate form of human production. This production, as all human thinking and making, contributes to our common evolving culture. A plumber finding new ways to install a sink, a farmer involved in agri-culture, as well as an artist carving a stone, are all creating our common culture. But art differs from other forms of human production in that it is a consequence of imagination concerned with beauty, truth and the nature of the human condition. Art, as opposed to decoration, crafts, entertainment and propaganda must, by its nature, be in opposition to the narrow acceptable canon of possibilities offered by the Establishment. Where I mention 'Establishment' I mean the richest 10% of the population who work to support the status quo and their positions within it.

LEARNING TO REFUSE

is one of the central problems artists have, which they share with the rest of humanity. They, as most people, have been regulated, canalized, restricted, intimidated, repressed, and forced by the schooling system, the surrounding popular culture and the deeply seated assumptions of corrupted democracies into developing a set of beliefs which they think to be original to themselves and good for them but which are, in reality, detrimental to them.

This has been called *'the creation of false consciousness'*.

How then can they free themselves from the auto-oppression deeply seared into their own individual character instincts? How can they successfully imagine the liberation of society until they can imagine the liberation of themselves?

This means that artists must be able to step back, see themselves inside the power and wealth relationships that engulf them, imagine *a radical subjectivity* and an immunity to defend that subjectivity in the face of almost total cultural and often political opposition.

This radical opposition needs to consist of resistance to all forms of injustice, unfairness, and the continual un-acceptance of intimidation and the material inducement of the Establishment. It means that often one must stand in the flood of history and shout *'NO'* to it and to all those who fill the upstream reservoirs with exploitation, wars and hatred. This in part constitutes what Herbert Marcuse called 'the great refusal'.

AUTHENTICITY

develops within the consciousness of experienced artists. It arises from working at and discovering the truths of one's self and truths within others. It is dependent on the survival of curiosity within the individual. As we may remember from our childhood, often parents and most often school systems seek to crush our wonderment, and to

silence our repeated 'why' this and 'why' that,
because to question is to threaten.

In our shared world of manufactured reality (a
reality now pieced together in the bowels of trans-
national media corporations), authenticity is
relegated to being a virtue of shallow heroes:
detectives, lawyers, soldiers or superheroes who are
often killers.

Without authenticity it is impossible to be a fulfilled
human being, and yet for many it is easier to turn
away from the revelations that might take them
towards an authentic life, a life redeemed from the
falsehoods we live within.

For an artist's practice, authenticity may come from
a deep understanding of the world, perhaps from a
vibrant emotional intelligence as well as from the
choices they make about what to show and what to
tell.

CONVICTION

suggests certainty, the certainty which comes from
witnessing enough of life that one begins to believe
that apple and emerald green are at least hues of
green, that kindness is about goodness rather than
weakness, that misrepresentations of the truth are
intentional and meant to delude us. Conviction
means that an artist is committed to the truth she
perceives and wishes to deliver to others, perhaps
hoping that in so doing, those others will take action
to bring change; but be aware that total
unquestioned conviction fosters fanaticism while
uncertainty suggests curiosity and perhaps wisdom.

AUTHORITY

comes from boldness that is a consequence of recognizing one's views and creative works have meaning and a positive effect upon people; that one's work help to influence consciousness bringing awareness and promoting change. It also implies that the individual has sufficient belief to stand forward in those moments of silence to speak their truths.

PRESENCE

in the creative process is the result of many of the above things and the amount of education, culture, experiences, thoughtfulness, sensibility and awareness one brings to bear upon each photograph or other creative invention. Presence begins in the initial thinking about themes and content, followed by considerations of form and technique. In making photographs, it ignites hyper awareness at the moment of releasing the shutter and during the time spent selecting, printing, perhaps writing captions or texts, until finally presenting the work to an audience. Presence comes from the time of one's life invested in the making of something.

TRUTH-TELLING

is a result of being committed to representing meaningful human experiences in all of its ages and impermanence, however modest or grand. In a period when truth itself is no longer treated as a virtue, to simply describe 'what is' carries the power to change people's perceptions. Truth-telling is not simply about an accurate rendering of the surface of things but rather about revealing the tensions between the inner and outer existence of people, events and social periods.

REDEMPTION

is to climb out of the pit of confusion and despair
amply spawned by corporate media's popular
culture; a culture which seeks to atomize individuals
and turn us into docile consumers.

Redemption allows us the ability to see our world
clearly and to be able to create stories that make
sense of it. For this we need to redeem our repressed
selves through our imaginations. It is not only a
matter of logic or reason, so much as a matter of
recovering lost dreams. Redemption is also an
exchange between the artist and the audience in that
the beauty of art can be a balm for sorrowful souls.

DIALOGUE

is a consequence of art. I have an exhibition worked
on for 11 years, printed, mounted and framed,
shown in four venues but now sitting in my
workroom, wrapped in plastic. There it has no
meaning because to have meaning it needs the eyes
of the audience, just as the novel needs the reader
and the opera needs the listener.

Why are the arts avoided by so many? Perhaps
because they are challenging to our fixed universe.
Ben Okri[vi] wrote *'books are a dialogue between souls'*.
So too are photographs and films, but only if the
books, photographs and films address the things
that have meaning to the audience and which
prompt dissatisfaction and change.

IMPERMANENCE

riddles our lives as a condition imposed upon us by
the fragmentation of contemporary culture and by

people being alienated from the consequences or products of their day-by-day work.

Impermanence can be challenged by the authenticity and authority of artists.

People in the past, who could afford to be photographed or painted, undertook these events with considerable attention and seriousness. Those portraits carried within them the inevitable sense of the sitter's own demise. That impermanence, combined with the burdens of life – both of power and poverty – more profoundly reflected a stable if not to say rigidified human condition. It also reflected a clear understanding of their place in a fixed universe of knowable spaces, duties and traditions.

Today's escapist culture and hyperactivity turn people away from their lost souls. Now portraits are often used to sell us life-style, idealised appearances whether through clothing, make-up or electronic consumer goods. Portraits show us how happy we will be when we borrow money, purchase a car or take out a mortgage. Sometimes these images shout at us; at other times they create emotional static by whispering to us how discontented we must be because we do not conform to corporate ideals. Although often filled with kinetic energy and beautiful specimens of our species, they are shallow, bereft of sincerity, truthfulness or a vital life force.

Consider the selfie, an inchoate plea for permanence in a destabilized world of human slaughter, climate change and warring strangers.

It begs for one to be noticed and accounted for, to prove one's ownership over a shard of digital space, over having been here or there, having consumed an event or a place, having been happy in other people's company. When have you seen a Selfie that touches your heart?

But, in difficult times, stasis, the opposite of impermanence, is always the enemy of progressive change because the dominant ideology attempts to impose upon the majority of people the notion that more of the same is a good thing.

REVELATION

rather than explanation is one of the tasks of art. Art does not explain – when it explains it becomes finger wagging, it slips into propaganda. Art explores and reveals.

When I look at or read any art form, I ask myself, *"have I been touched by this? Has it informed my humanity? Has it increased my understanding of what it is to be a decent human being, to be able to understand the rigors of life, to find empathy for the condition of others? Has the pursuit of the artist, no matter the style, the subject matter or the apparent theme, been to reveal truths relevant to our time? And can I see or hear harmony between the artist's personal pursuits of form and/or of narrative with the needs of our time?"*

This primary inquiry: *'is the work relevant to our time'* is always central to my response. Even when I say to myself that the work is clever or entertaining, I separate that from whether it has touched my heart, or had allowed me to see greater depths and wider

horizons, and has especially helped me to engage
my own humanity. In the simplest terms – has it
served me to become wiser, kinder, more motivated
to struggle for change?

This is not a superficial demand that art must
conform to specific social/political idea, that it
'serves the revolution', that 'it explains the moment'.
That would be to demand that art is actually meant
to be propaganda.

Art is subtle, poetic, generous, multi-layered,
nuanced, often indirect and it offers a dialogue,
asking questions of the reader or viewer.

Propaganda is strict, demanding subservience,
insisting on a singular truth and it is clearly does not
offer a discussion but makes a proclamation.

Art works on more profound layers of our
consciousness. Those that touch us more deeply we
harbour for the rest of our lives.

Caravaggio, Leonardo, Michelangelo, Rembrandt,
and yes, many photographers including Paul Strand,
W. Eugene Smith and Edward Weston are always a
part of me, as are Mozart, Aaron Schoenberg, Garcia
Lorca, Nazim Hikmet and Albert Camus.

They are irresistible.

THE VALUE OF ART
is not only in the particular work but also in the way
the audience may perceive the artist's way of
looking at our troubled world.

If I do not sense dignity - a kind of intellectual and creative nobility, if I can only understand self-indulgence – that middle-class preoccupation with their every sneeze and every passing emotion, or as is usual, their preoccupation with the 'I' over the 'We', that is if I sense their individualism run amuck is more important than their care for others, I am left emptied, sullied by their ego-centrism and my waste of time.

This 'I' centred preoccupation is a lazy capitulation to the acceptable cultural conformity of our time. It is an embrace of the status quo and in the case of most of this production, it is questionably called 'art' rather than more realistically called 'entertainment' or 'decoration'. It creates diversions; a celebration of the monetary value of an unmade bed or a diamond covered skull rather than a tender embrace of our struggling human spirit.

For me, I conclude that if the work does not raise within me a need for change, a drive to engage with others, a celebration for developing our common humanity, it has no value whatsoever.
Recently a doctor said to me that you are not what you eat but rather you are what you digest. It is the same for how creative work is actually digested by us.

Why 500 years after Leonardo or 100 years after Schoenberg or 50 years after Albert Camus and 30 years after W. Eugene Smith do their works still carry meaning for me? It is because inherent to the form and content of what they did is not only formal

beauty but an embrace of my humanity and for that
I have an enduring love.

SUMMARY

• If art does not represent the needs of some sector of
the general population there will be few people
interested in it. The artist will not have an audience
for his/her self-preoccupations except perhaps
amongst a group of friends. Without relevance to
other's lives why would people use their precious
time or pay to see it?

• It is vital that artists are intellectually or
emotionally mature enough to sense and respond to
the concerns of the community in which they live. If
not, they cannot represent or address their needs.

• To be able to address others and their own needs,
they must see clearly the nature of wealth and
power, which causes the inequality, poverty, illness,
hunger, injustices and hopelessness of others.

• But artists, as all of us, cannot see clearly from
inside the system that oppresses us. The artist must
be prepared to step outside the assumptions of the
dominant ideology.

• The artist must be curious, ornery and prepared to
shout 'NO' to all repression and all conventions
while at the same time, accepting it is likely that as
they reject the system, the system's guardians will
reject them. Goodbye to wealth and fame, hello
dignity, self-respect and the ability to represent
alternative truths consistent with the needs of the
world's oppressed.

• I will say this now and repeat it later: that there
cannot be a prescription for what makes fine and
meaningful art that communicates with others. I

believe what I have said above is broadly true and suits my practice, just as others find different ways. But one cannot produce in ignorance.

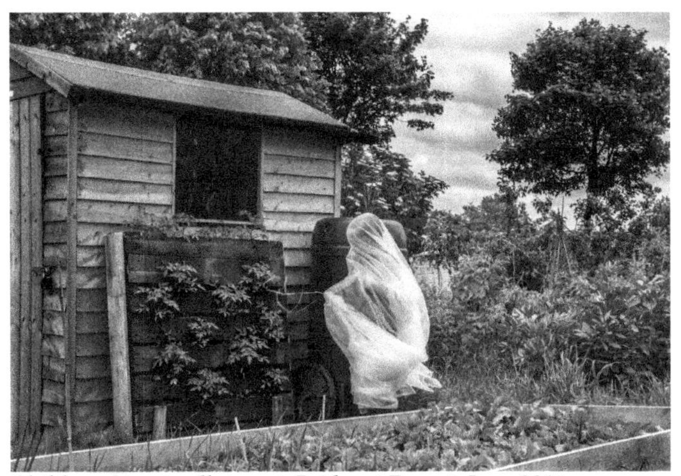

Child running in allotment, Bridport Dorset, June 2016;
photograph: Robert Golden

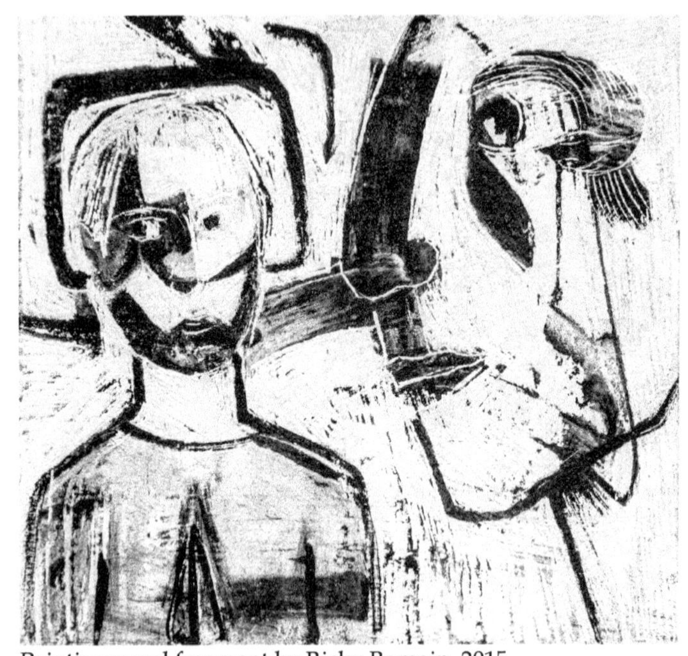

Painting panel fragment by Ricky Romain, 2015

4

A ROLE FOR ARTISTS
IN TROUBLED TIMES

WHAT IS THIS ROLE FOR ART?

Because I have seen many sorts of suffering and injustice and because, when others suffer or are diminished, we are all diminished. I want my grandchildren and yours to have a life in a stable and beautiful peaceful world and to not inherit a Brexited Britain, a Trumped US and a tortured Syria; and because I do not want our children to be shot in the streets or hunted down like my distant relatives, or like the children of Yemen, or to drown while sailing for a life without fear, and because I want them to live in truth, with knowledge and beauty being their common language with others, I believe that only art will save us and them from continually stumbling into hell while on our collective journey during these unnecessarily difficult times.

Am I blind to the financial and moral corruption that seeps into the crevice of public and commercial life? Am I dumb to the lazy ignorance and lies of our leaders? Am I deaf to the sounds of their bombs and guns used around the world to control their global interests? Can I not taste the poisoned air as they destroy Gaia?

I know these things, as do most of you, but I have seen this: that whatever we think we know of our political and economic failure and how injurious it and the ultra-wealthy and their Establishment have been to collective social life, most of us still don't get

99

it: that our best interests are not in the least the best
interests of the Establishment. They encircle us with
their ideological prejudices using their popular
culture. They stifle us within their oppressive school
systems. They bombard us with their distorted
telling of the news, and they mislead us with their
election circuses - all in order to do what?

Primarily, they wish to have us acquiesce to working
longer hours for less and less wages in order to
produce greater profits for them. The 'what', in its
most naked form, is to more intensively exploit our
labour for their wealth. Secondarily they wish to
destroy the welfare state and our resistance to this
destruction so they may privatise everything whilst
diminishing the size of the state.

Over the last thirty-eight years they have increased
our taxes and basic expenses, reduced our wages
relative to the cost of living and to the profits we
make for them per hour of our work, and have
reduced their financial support for the welfare state.

All of this required changing our belief systems and
forsaking many underlying principles of fairness
and justice. Through advertising and public
relations messages, and by taking over the internet,
they have convinced many of us to imagine
ourselves as consumers rather than producers; to be
'I' centred rather than 'we' embracing; to buy into
their consumer society[vii] whilst we enslave ourselves
with their trinkets and our over-used credit cards;
and to reject our communal history in favour of
individual psychology.

In our silence and our embarrassment of making a fuss, we allow the politicians to act in their own self-interest, and to act for the wealthiest .01% of people hiding behind the curtain, those who secretly pay for the politician's election campaigns.

We allow them to act in our names whilst perpetrating injustices at home and around the globe. We allow them to roll over us with their obsessive avarice while destroying all that is decent and beautiful. We turn away as they serve, not our young who die in their armies, not the old who need support, not the worker who needs a decent income, not any of us who need to live in truth, but the needs of corporate capitalism. Our silence grants them freedom to oppress others and us.

When artists protest that they are not political, they are in fact saying, *"my complacency, my inactivity, my disinterest is my submission to their rule; my inaction is a vote for the status quo. My inactivity supports their oppression of me."*

As I write, there are exciting social and cultural experiments occurring around the world; things we hear little of because positive stories provide examples of resistance and change. Within cultural activity, and, in particular, within the arts - as a specific form of culture - there are projects that act as powerful tools capable of changing hearts and minds towards higher ideals of love, kindness, humility, knowledge, freedom and empathy.

Those tools can only be in the hands of artists who have said *'no'* to the status quo, who have decided they cannot comfortably fit into the narrow economic and cultural traps which capitalism offers them. Those who are free of the marketplace, and free of its assumptions and distortions remain capable of curiosity. This allows them to create outside the popular culture's narrow restrictions; restrictions that defeat most people. For these reasons alone, artists are precious oracles of our social and political futures.

That is why I wish to discuss a role for artists in these troubled times. I know that art is one of the truly positive transformative human journeys we can hitch a ride with, that may help to draw a line under bigotry, nationalism, elitism and the sundry hatreds so cleverly encouraged by the dominant culture of the global elites.

THE UNIQUE VALUE OF ART

Many people have said that in a time like this, *"art is meaningless, art does not stop wars nor does it feed people"*.

Those on the side of power who understand the potential of art, are rightfully frightened of it because they know it is not meaningless, but rather one of the few human activities that can inform and change people's worldview.

When alien armies invade another country or take power from within a country, the first arrests are of the rare un-purchasable politicians, rebellious trade unionists, recalcitrant journalists and finally the artists.[viii]

Why the artists? Because if they are true artists – not decorators, not entertainers, not sycophants - but irascible, rebellious, anti-authoritarian, questioning, curious people with a vision of what is and what could be, they will always offer a reminder of one's humanity, or a vision of a better world, or solace and comradeship, or an understanding that those who suffer are not alone. If nothing else, they may offer a frank description of their shared sullied world.

All of the above are a threat to those with power and wealth because the very nature of true art is an offer to replace suffering with a better life and a better world. Great art often offers hope, or at least a deep understanding of one's plight.

The second thing an alien force does is to destroy the art of the past, replacing it with a new quasi-art[ix] which celebrates the new rulers and their new oppressive narrative. They know that within a well-told cultural history our identity can be found.

True that art cannot directly feed the belly nor directly end wars, but it can feed souls that struggle against the avarice and hatreds that create hunger and fear.

"ENIGMA OF CREATION"

George Steiner, the linguist and philosopher wrote, *"that one of the defining tasks of this sombre age is to learn anew to be human"*.

He went on to say that a vital part of this is comprised of coming to appreciate and experience the *'enigma of creation'* as discovered in music, dance, indeed in all the arts. This embraces the necessity, vitality and thus the role of the arts in our world

All art arises from the individual but the source of their knowledge, culture, tastes, preoccupations and their experiences are not of them alone but of their family, friends, neighbourhood, city and broader culture from which they come. Their psyche is not a free-floating angel's feather but a consciousness originally anchored in and born out of the surrounding societies' ways of making a life out of bamboo or iron, out of cotton or wool, out of fire and water and with wheat or rice.

More important is that one's morality and ethical boundaries are anchored there. It is where we learn how we struggle to become humane, which is essential to create an art of meaning and relevance for the artist's potential audience.

All great art flows from the particular to the general, from the substances of a social setting, via the artists and their art, to others, and perhaps to others beyond their immediate farm, village or city to become universal.

Courbet and other painters arose from the peasantry and intimately knew of their pain and their wiles. The desire to be a part of and to escape from such backgrounds created tensions that invariably are revealed in their work. It is these tensions which lead to drama and to revelations and it is these which make their work outstanding.

ART AS MEMORY

When I think of the late 15th to early 16th century Renaissance in Florence, I don't at first recall the names of battles or generals, nor do I easily recall which of the Medici were then ruling the roost of power.

How do I remember that period? By remembering the drawings of Leonardo Da Vinci, *The Slaves* of Michelangelo, and the portraits of Raphael.

How do I remember the fall of the aristocracy and the rise of the middle-classes in post revolutionary Amsterdam of the 17th century? By remembering the late self-portraits of Rembrandt.

And for the beginning of the 20th century, before I recall Henry Ford, Thomas Edison and Rockefeller, I think of Cezanne, Matisse, Picasso, and the music of Schoenberg and Satie.

For being supposedly ineffectual, art has a power over our memories and our characterization of the past.

Consider this: that the belief system of the middle and ruling classes, that is, their neoliberal[x] ideology serves to guide them. It also serves to befuddle the rest of us as it disguises our past. We can only know ourselves if we understand the needs and wants of the people from where we came. The politicos, academics, intellectuals and powerful moneyed interests of the middle classes know that to obscure our history hides from us the actions of others who

have made us what we are. The consequential
emptiness has led to the rebirth, especially amongst
the young, of nihilism.

If nihilism is about one thing, it is hopelessness[xi].
Today, after these many years of Neoliberal policies
gutting beauty and intelligence from our culture and
traditions, while swamping them with empty
materialism and an infantile popular culture, the
neoliberal establishment has constructed a
mental/emotional landscape without meaningful
goals, without inspiring heroes, and without hope
for a better, relevant and fulfilling life. This crime of
stealing from all of us, but particularly from stealing
the dreams of the young, is compounded by the
extension of their ideas into the spheres of
international politics, economics and culture.

As the singer/song writer Don Mclean wrote in his
famous song, *Vincent*:
> *"now I understand what you tried to say to me*
> *and how you suffered for your sanity*
> *and how you tried to set them free;*
> *they would not listen,*
> *they would not know how,*
> *perhaps they'll listen now...*
> *but I could have told you Vincent*
> *this world was not made for someone as*
> *beautiful as you."*

If it is one thing that the endlessly compromising
middle classes with their shifting sands morality do
not have is Vincent's beauty.

LEARNING HUMANITY

Steven Pinker's book, *The Better Angels Of Our Nature,* reveals and proves statistically - as difficult as it may seem - that the sanctity of each individual human life has been increasingly valued since the Renaissance. Beginning with Dante and his epic *Divine Comedy* of the early 14th century, people have learned the value of their individuality through poetry and art. Dante gave God an excuse to leave centre stage to humanity. It was neither in the interests of the church nor the ruling classes to help people understand their value and distinctiveness. That happened only through the arts and through moments of rebellious uprisings.

After the Renaissance, artists no longer had to depict people as vague reflections of an assumed holy spirit but could see them for what they were – individuals with a character and with a real physical and yes with a sexual existence, having physical flaws and human foibles.

Pinker's book proves that the number of people tortured, killed or maimed by other individuals and slaughtered in wars, even despite the horrors of the last century and the continual mayhem of this one, in proportion to the total world population the percentage of those deaths continually drops.

He reminds us that the in mid-17th century Age Of Enlightenment, John Locke[xii], challenged the divine rights of kings and their absolute monarchies as he proposed that all 'men' had a natural right to life, liberty and property. Throughout the last 375 years these ideas spread across the Western world and beyond, becoming central to the social contract between citizens and their governments.

As many ideas, these too have become distorted by real world pressures. In particular, their natural political consequence – Democracy - has been captured and then corrupted by capitalism's creation of poverty and inequality. Life and liberty have lost out to property. This unleashed human frailty in the form of murderous avarice and greed, both of which have so forcefully been pursued by those who would rise through the middle classes to become masters of society.

How contradictory are these controls to what we imagine Democracy should be? George Orwell, the English author of 1984, *Animal Farm* and many other visionary novels and articles, said that what is dangerous for our rulers is not the supposed existence of Democracy, but rather people's belief in and hope for its values. In other words, it is the gap between our belief in a fair and just system and what we actually live within that creates an existential threat to the wealthy.

As globalisation and austerity have pushed people to their limits, it has also increased the number of people beginning to challenge the way Capitalism and the Establishment make wars and create famine, disregard climate change and encourage increasing inequality, racism and sexism. As has been said *"in the grip of defeat or terrible tragedy, you can kill the person but not the idea"*. This is often communicated to people by their artists.

John Berger, British artist, writer and critic, talked about how artists may recognise they have become discontented by celebrating the property and position of the rich who are their natural financial patrons. With this recognition they begin to question their art. Here is where form, content and technique become subjected to curiosity, self-doubt, and perhaps even recrimination as the artist begins to understand that his or her position is, as I later address, *"a fungus growing on the loam of the injured and dead victims of their patron's wealth and power"*.

This means that the artist must call to question the traditions of their art (the cultural canons) that have brought him/her to where they are. The unity between their success amongst middleclass audiences, the traditions and the values of truthfulness, originality and beauty are thus open to questions. This is the shaft of light that may lead to truly inspiring work.

It is interesting to think of Caravaggio's paintings and Eugene Smith's photographs with the above in mind. Each of these image-makers placed their subject matter within shadows and darkness. Perhaps they were doing so to dismiss the influence of backgrounds, decorated walls and artefacts that provide a description of context or distract from the intensity and drama of the foreground. In either case, these two artists lived in continual opposition to the cultural canon of their day. The viewer can recognise truths emerging from darkness.

People are beginning to resist because a scattering of brave philosophers, a few social leaders, a handful of courageous journalists and artists have had the facts, knowledge and wisdom, the depth of perception and a well of humanity to imaginatively create work that has questioned and at times undermined authority. Over the long haul of history, they have helped many others to recognise the rightfulness of equality, the insanity of war and the need to constantly remind us of the values of truth, beauty and love.

This is one of the most important roles for art and artists.

FUNGI GROWING IN THE LOAM OF THE DEAD

"There is no document of civilization which is not at the same time a document of barbarism."
John Berger[xiii] from *Landscapes*

I have had the luxury to construct humanist sensitivities on the back of monsters who rape, pillage, destroy and eviscerate all that is fine in life for millions if not billions of our brothers and sisters.

This is a white Euro-American humanism whose believers, like myself, must recognise that our ethics and morality are the fungi growing in the loam of the dead. It is one of the inescapable, sorrowful truths of our history, a history in which even our better thoughts are a consequence if not victims to the terrifying power of the Neoliberal establishment's day-by-day horror show.

This is to recognise that people in need, people in struggle, people exploited, impoverished and set against each other can hardly remember that once, people like them, their grandparents for instance, embraced an ethos of solidarity and working class consciousness, a consciousness now drowning in greed, consumption and debt, which allows for hardly a glimmer of a better future.

We grasp the present through the past. We have nothing else. But the present is too present to understand itself and we are too smothered in its images, its chatter, lies and gossip to know better.

We need the comparison of collective history, the memory of being human, of at least holding dear other people's dreams of a good life.

Certainly the past can be recalled in books as well as in paintings and photographs, or retold by our elders if we care to listen, and at times these shards of culture strike us like shooting stars, illuminating what we have become in relation to what we once were: innocents lying on our backs imagining the clouds as monsters, virgins touching the skin of our first infatuation, idealists dreaming of a better more dignified world. For a moment it is like falling in love or finally witnessing what we have become.

True art (not decoration, not entertainment) gives meaning to life. It provides a voice for the voiceless; it gives form to the establishment's hidden agenda; it makes the invisible visible; it offers an emotional crust to fill hungry souls, souls gutted by the meaningless, ugly, banal popular culture which stuffs us with a cotton candy of false consciousness and a confused morality.

This is why it is vital to link one's art with a clear analysis of the surrounding horror; this is why we need to continually examine not only the splendour of creativity but its function and utility in the struggle to make a better world.

It is never a coincidence that artists and rebels are often allies if indeed not the same person.

A PERSONAL NOTE

To produce art, which has the power to stop wars and to feed people, I need to know what I need to know and what tools I must have. Whilst economics and politics are rigidified in the hands of a powerful elite, art, which is in our hands, is malleable. In itself, in its processes alone or in groups, it is possibly transformative of consciousness and beliefs – that is why it has the power to stop wars and to feed people.

First I must ask this: 'is my foremost task that I need to light the lamp of reason and search my soul for who I am, and then do I need to ask what it is I know and how I know what I think to be true, is true?"

As a photographer and film-maker I know I need to ask:
•What is the role of my work in my personal and social life? Is it about fame and fortune, or creating a better world?
•Does this search demand that I investigate my relationship to my personal and social truths?

• And if I recognise that I, or my work, has an effect upon the consciousness of others, how then do I understand my obligations, if any, to those others?
• Or is it a valid role to decorate and entertain while receiving payment from those who oppress others and myself?

This may sound complicated, but be patient and I'll try to unwind these things. Simply said, this is about how I concern myself with kindness, with the care of others, with my adherence or inattention to the conditions of my own soul and my preservation of dignity, self-respect, and all of that in relation to the society in which I live.

Before I continue I want to tell you a short story about some things I have experienced, not because I think I am especially interesting but because the experiences explain something critical about how I, and probably others, come to construct beliefs.

In my first year of university I was nominated for a scholarship by a group of leftist academics. It would have sent me to Harvard or Yale...places I could little afford on my own. The day after my nomination I was listening to a lecture amongst about a hundred other students when I was physically attacked by a right wing teaching fellow who was also a judo expert. Even with 30 witnesses attesting to the fact that he launched this assault on me, I was kicked out of the university and of course lost the scholarship, which was the point of the attack.

I realised that I meant nothing; I could have been anyone. What had meaning to the Right was that a nominee of the Left should not receive the benefit of such a prestigious award.

Because I was a good student academically I had to be accepted by the University of Michigan as an in-state student. The first day of the new school year I entered the English class and as I settled down an official entered and demanded that *"Golden shows himself"*. I stood up as he snapped, *"You, you're out of here, I'm taking you to the dean."*

Disregarding my grades and my results on intelligence tests, I was told that I should leave the university and go to a farmer's college, as I was not academic material.

I survived the intimidation and stayed. Needless to say, I was radicalised. Later that year I went to Montgomery Alabama with about 20 other students to answer a call by Martin Luther King to help bring the world's press to the region. This was because, after the violence of the first Selma march, the second Selma march was about to take place. We, about 80 of us from different universities around the country, were asked to carry a petition to the racist governor, George Wallace, demanding that the second march should, under the law, be allowed to happen in peace.

We were attacked by the Ku Klux Klan (KKK) on horseback welding crowbars with claw hammers tied to them, and by state troopers on motorcycles, driving through us at speed. I met my first wife under a bucking KKK horse.

Later that day, those of us still able to stand were
asked to go to a small wooden church in the black
community. After we arrived, Martin Luther King
showed up. Soon we realised that this tiny wooden
church was surrounded by torch carrying KKK on
horseback and by a phalanx of state troopers. There
was no escape. Hours later the surrounding black
community realised what was going on and came
out of their houses – men, women, children,
grandparents and friends. They surrounded the
KKK and the troopers who quickly faded away.

Since those days, I have photographed and been part
of many demonstrations, riots, marches, anti-Nazi
blockades, even taking part in a vicious pub brawl
with skinhead Nazis. I lost clients because I would
not cross picket lines; I have told editors I did not
like my images being used to conform to their
owner's racist or other right wing views. I have
filmed around the world and seen in the eyes of too
many people the actual reality of globalization ... the
heartless and pernicious expansion of Anglo-
American capitalism over the last 43 years.

These things are real to me. They are visceral and
live in the memory of so many images I've made,
and in the cracked voices of so many interviewees
and in the body language of so many distressed
people.

Even if you disagree with the way I construct my
ideas about the necessity of art, the responsibility of
artists and what it means to be not only an artist but
a good and responsible citizen and neighbour,
please accept that they are constructed not alone on

abstractions but on having asked, *"what can I do to help others, how can I serve and what is my responsibility???"*

THE ESSENTIAL JOURNEY

Here is a parable to consider: We take a journey. At first we are carried by our parents on a road that twists through a dense, dark forest. Our parents or others seek a path by holding their lanterns high, looking for the easiest and least dangerous way. Eventually we totter behind and soon we walk and after, we stride shoulder to shoulder with others of our generation. Finally we take the lanterns from our elders and seek the path ourselves as we support them.

That is what history is. A series of events connected by a common cause, a common story to seek a better life, to find love and to always hope, to discover a meaning in one's existence. We are guided and formed by it and our community until we ourselves unwittingly become the guides.

If we have no idea where we come from, where we are and where we may wish to go, we float in a miasma of confusion honed by those who wish us to serve them. Our uncertainty and confusion make it easier for the rulers to victimise us.

The word 'history' has two roots in ancient Greek – one meaning 'to see', and the other meaning 'to know'. In its best and most exciting sense it is not to 'entertain', but to help you 'see and know'.

If we do not see and know our history, if we do not know how we got to where we are, if we do not know where we are on our path and where it's leading, if we do not understand who controls what we are or what our imaginations are free to access, and if we do not know how it is that we have little and others have a lot, how can we produce any art of value to help others?

When we are young we strive to understand, we gather facts and eventually these facts form opinions –which we refer to as *'knowledge'*. And as we become older, experiencing the vagaries of life, witnessing the pain of ourselves and other's living and dying, perhaps we come to see life as did Albert Camus[xiv] – in that at its core is the tragedy that our spirit/soul/psyche wishes to survive whilst our bodies are programmed to wear and die. This leads some to form wisdom out of knowledge, a way of understanding and perhaps accepting our common fate but rejecting our common oppression.

Sensing and feeling, caring and compassion, sympathy and empathy and all the tears that dampen my cheeks are vital but not enough.

THE NEED TO UNDERSTAND

A Hungarian Marxist art critic of the first half of the 20th century named Georg Lukács, daringly stood against Russian Soviet Socialist Realist art[xv] by supporting Western humanist instincts[xvi].

In Lukács's late book on literature, *The Meaning Of Contemporary Realism*, he wrote that Western middle class artists are overly concerned with the importance of every sneeze they make. He pointed out that their Naturalism is single dimensional, concerned only with the surface of events and with the appearance of things, while Realism is multidimensional (and in his terms, dialectical,) in that it reveals both the inner personal and external social reality of its characters.

Lukács argued that this new historical realism allowed novelists (and other artists) to describe their contemporary social life *"not as a static drama of fixed, universal types, but rather as a moment of history, constantly changing, open to the potential of revolutionary transformation"*.

Through the conflict of a character's inner needs and outer pressures, there is created a natural and understandable tension, a tension that leads to drama. This broader and deeper understanding of character is more revealing of lived life – of how the inner self is affected and in turn affects the external world.

For me, this realism is not a prescription. It is simply a way to grasp what is real and in particular, to picture the vital link between our inner and other worlds and the importance of both. It is not so much a style as a way of thinking, a mode of comprehending a complex and difficult existence in the midst of endless conflict.

All of the above drew me again and again to this: how did I wind up believing what I believe, and why do I think that what I believe is true? When I say 'true' what I mean is that I hope that my always present and always active subjectivity is more rather than less closely aligned to whatever we measure or define as measurable objective truth[xvii].

Before I go on to discuss art itself I need to point out a few more things that get in the way for many being able to create work which addresses other's needs.

> *"One day we must ask the question:*
> *Why are there 40 million poor people in America (and*
> *why is 33% of the British population) below the*
> *poverty line?*
>
> *And when you begin to ask that question, you are*
> *raising questions about the economic system,*
> *about a broader distribution of wealth. When*
> *you ask that question, you begin to question the*
> *capitalist economy. And I'm simply saying*
> *that more and more, we've got to begin to ask*
> *questions about the whole society...*
> *What I am saying to you ... is that Communism*
> *forgets that life is individual.*
> *Capitalism forgets life is social, and the*
> *Kingdom of Brotherhood is found neither*
> *in the thesis of Communism nor in*
> *the antithesis of capitalism but... in a higher synthesis*
> *that combines the truths of both.*
> *Now, when I say 'question the whole society',*
> *it means ultimately coming to see that*
> *the problems of racism, the problems*
> *of economic exploitation, and the problems of war*
> *are all tied together.*
> *These are the triple evils that are interrelated."*

Eight months after Martin Luther King delivered the above in a speech, eight months after he had begun to question both capitalism and imperialism, on April the 4th, 1968, he was shot dead. (speech given on August 16, 1967)

The 38 year old oppressive system we now live within, Neoliberalism, having refused to share new wealth extracted by globalization, has left billions of people in destitution, and in the Anglo-American world, has left millions jobless or on low wages, with poor education and without hope.

In the slowly emerging shadows, the new racist demagogues have festered and have begun to thrive.

The refusal of the neoliberals to accept that wealth must be shared has unwittingly stage-managed the rise of the Right whose cunning use of cultural tools, single dimensional stories and simplistic slogans have proven to be their most effective weapons.

CHANGING CONSCIOUSNESS

Brexit, Trump and carrion flocks of other populists in the broken branches of their simplistic popular culture offer answers wrapped in Hallmark card emotions: racism, fear and hatred of foreigners, a supposed love of one's own people and country and contempt for all others; an unstated willingness to use violence to reach their goals; a preoccupation with supposed heroic masculine values which are actually degenerate macho ravings; an embrace of un-investigated sacred cow-like ideals while proudly wearing post-factual ignorance on their lapels accompanied by contempt for a free press, intelligence, art and intellectualism. These are emerging shadows of past darkness and murder. Why this? Why now?

> *"The reality today is that we live in a democratic society defined by a*
> *commerce that is anything but*
> *democratic, but is tyrannising,*
> *homogenising, corrupting,*
> *commodifying, debasing, depreciating,*
> *infantilising, and is an instrument of the single-*
> *minded, dehumanised obsession*
> *with profit, money and materialism."*
> Benjamin Barber[xviii] – American cultural critic

A part of the Neoliberal plan to convince the middle classes to accept this new cage, was to slowly change our habits and consciousness from thinking of ourselves as a collective of producers with a community conscience, into thinking of ourselves as competitive individual consumers, whose central preoccupation was no longer the health of our communities but the size of our house, car and bank account.

This atomization was planned to separate individuals from each other as a way to break the communal idea of unions. Not only has this changed the sense of who we are but has also led to endless consumption as the main component of identity and as a driver of a junk economy that must continually grow or die.

It was clear to the Neoliberals that neither police nor military forces on their own nor providing only basic financial survival would work to secure the on-going political dominance of the .01%. They decided[xix] to boost material wants via advertising as a diversion from the real problems of life and as a way to further create indebtedness for the middle class and greater wealth for themselves. Indebtedness encourages docility in the workplace because of people's fear of losing their jobs and with them, their things and homes. As Benjamin Barber later wrote:

> *"The new capitalism does not manufacture goods to meet real needs; it manufactures needs (via its corporate made popular culture and advertising) to sell all the goods it has."*

This is why they are keen to finance advertising during TV and radio programmes and in newspapers and on-line. Those stories and programmes they sponsor feed the people with the advertiser's manufactured needs.

This new culture brought together many economic threads proffered by Reagan and Thatcher under Neoliberal influence. In particular, it encouraged the formation of larger but fewer media corporations[xx] while disregarding the spirit of US anti-trust laws and the UK's Office of Communication's (OFCOM) regulatory guidelines.

This purposeful ignorance of the spirit of the law in both countries was undertaken to create a new set of values within the popular culture. The new media giants would more easily construct and spread them, having gained unprecedented controls over culture and the news.

Eventually harnessing the increasing power of computers to gather information from the web, they have been able to create individualised echo chambers appealing to each person's perceived tastes constructed from the on-line clicks we make, and in this way to develop 'Perception Management' – a way of constructing not only what we think we know but also how we think we know it. The more we are intertwined with these echoes, the more they inform what we think are our free choices.

Read Richard Condon's novel *The Manchurian Candidate* or see the 1962 film of the book to understand how this misapprehension of reality is encouraged by brainwashing[xxi].

It was these media corporation's task to form a superficial, wealth and celebrity oriented infantilised popular culture. They used their new power to emphasis a 'Me' centred individualism; to replace our common history with private psychology and to dumb down the general level of thought. Meanwhile they pushed the so-called 'freedom of personal consumption' as a simplistic alternative to the notions of collectivism and trade unionism. This newly celebrated individualism was 'cool'.

All of this was accompanied by encouraging suspicion of trade unions, civil rights lawyers and leaders, artists and intellectuals who revealed unpalatable truths to power. The popular culture either sneers, belittles or ignores them as time wasters, troublemaking-deviant-elitists with no 'practical' grip on what matters to the people (in the demeaned imaginations of the corporations): money, fame and power. Those best fitted to offer an alternative point of view were and are marginalised, shutting down any real debate over important ideas.

Via the insistence of advertising and the new giant media corporation's culture, 'Stuff' took over from 'Meaning' or you could say, materialism took over from the needs of the psyche.

Whilst I was filming a story in the Romanian countryside, I spoke with an uneducated but bright peasant farmer about the differences of living under communism and capitalism. He smiled and said, *"under Communism, if I whispered in a bread line that I was tired of having to wait for food, the next day the police would be knocking at my door. But now, under Capitalism I can go to the centre of my village and shout that I have no money for bread, and you know what? Nobody bothers to respond."*

He went on to say the difference is this, *"under communism man exploits man, but under capitalism it's just the opposite".*

THE GRADUALNESS OF HISTORY

Years ago a friend of mine was asked to institute a redesign of the Financial Times. He was to take another designer's overall plan and break it down to 1000 changes. Every day for three years he instituted one of those changes. By the end of the third year the paper looked entirely different.
As the editors suspected, no one knew when the changes began. It was as if somehow the changes

had occurred before the reader's eyes, but without them recognizing how or when they happened.

This is how we missed seeing the Neoliberal cage constructed around us. At no single change did we recognise this new policy or that new sell-off of the rail or the post office or even privatising army units and prisons were a part of the long-term systematic construction to entrap us in ignorance and poverty. Gradually they left us incapable of finding common ground with each other or of standing united against the Neoliberals, their bureaucrats and armed enforcers.

> *"I saw men didn't want to be saved from themselves, for that would mean they'd have to give up greed, and they'll never pay that price for liberty. So I said to the world, god bless all here, and may the best man win and die of gluttony!"*
> The Ice Man Cometh
> by Eugene O'Neill[xxii]

HIRING SERVANTS

Under Democracy, just as under Stalinism, many academics, intellectuals, journalists and artists believe the status quo is good or at least a viable alternative or, as the servants they become within the Establishment, they gladly accept wealth and fame in exchange for their talents to serve the status quo.

It becomes their role to filter what can and can't be said in the media; to day-by-day choose and frame the news; to decide who is to be celebrated and who is to be marginalised and who is to act as popular examples of achievement and success.

Ask yourself, when was the last time you witnessed a 'famous' person with a truly alternative point of view being honoured, celebrated and hosted on the popular media? In the US it has taken years for the mainstream news to acknowledge the existence of Bernie Sanders and yet still now, they show reluctance to cover his road show of political events.

It is these servant's job to define the educational syllabus destined to turn out alienated state-school-automatons who become industry's button pushers, bureaucracy's yes/no clones and compliant soldiers, while public schools (meaning private schools in the US) turn out trusted servants to inherit control of corporations and the Neoliberal state.

Tragically there are many synonyms to describe what the Neoliberals want our schools to produce: compliance, obedience, docility, submissiveness, deference, and yes, fearfulness and dreamlessness.

Remember, the culture we are now surrounded by no longer springs from the farms and coal mines, nor even from the universities and independent minds, but from the bowels of trans-national media corporations and state owned broadcasters like the BBC, all of whom have a vested interest in things staying the same.

Artists and writers, film-makers and production companies approach the corporate media like supplicants at the portals of their gods (often money), seeking approval for their projects. If given, the creators are surrounded by lawyers, producers, editors and their guidelines, that force the supplicants to conform to the ideas of the media's masters (the needs of the .01%). This is why nothing but mainstream trivia is ultimately made. Interesting, meaningful and relevant ideas are strained through Neoliberal cultural and political filters – that is, through their Cultural Canon[xxiii].

I approached the BBC with a project to relate how 200 international food corporations produce both starvation and obesity at the same time on different continents. The top dog producer I met listened to me and then said, *"I like shopping at Waitrose."* Thinking I had not been clear I repeated, *"it is not only about a single supermarket chain but the whole system that is responsible for death by starvation, everyday of the year of more than 95,000 children."*

He smiled and said, *"it's not in our interest"*. Incredulous and at a loss for words I stammered, *"are you saying the painful prolonged deaths of 95,000 children everyday of every year is not a story the BBC should tell?"* He smiled again.

Recently Police Commissioner Cressida Dick, the head of Scotland Yard, criticised hypocritical middle-class cocaine users who express concern about fair trade, climate change and our denatured food, but whose widespread use of cocaine fuels mayhem, murders and other violence in the streets of London and in the developing world, especially amongst poorer people.

Both of these stories reveal the contradictions between the stated morality of the middle classes and the actuality of their actions. What became clear to me was that I might be commissioned to make a film about a particular burger corporation, but I could not reveal the corrupt, law-breaking practices that underpin the international food system. What Commissioner Dick may have recognised was that she and her department are facing something more profound than law breaking but rather a deep social condition, one of a whole classes' malaise and self-deception.

Recall that it is always the role of journalists and artists to ask questions and when necessary to subvert the bully, the authoritarian and the repressive. If they do not do this they becomes servants of the Establishment and as such they become the Establishment's tool to propagandise the rest of us. In that case the journalists and artists do not produce multifaceted, rich and liberating works, but decorations, fantasies and superficial entertainment –things that obscure the truth or divert our attention. They are like the magician who waves the rabbit with his left hand whilst pouring the elixir of numbness into our beer glass with his right hand.

If you reject the nature of present day reality, meaning you find the morality and values of the dominant ideology unacceptable to your understanding of what it is to be a human being, then you can only rely upon history and culture to provide a framework and a way to understand the future. This is not to suggest that artists must study

history nor must have particular admiration for art
and culture, but rather to embrace them as signs of
what was once a celebration of our humanity rather
than a suburban titillation of our bedroom life.

> *"By definition (an artist) cannot put himself*
> *today in the service of those who make history;*
> *if he is at the service of those who suffer it.*
> Albert Camus' speech at the Nobel Banquet
> at the City Hall, Stockholm; December 10, 1957

These manifestations of culture - <u>their</u> stories with
<u>their</u> points of view, with <u>their</u> underlying values
add up to the creation of <u>their</u> cultural canon, which
forms <u>their</u> set of cultural rules.

All of <u>their</u> radio and TV broadcasts, <u>their</u> films and
published novels carry <u>their</u> messages to our hearts
and minds, messages they surround us with from
childhood, seducing us into accepting a set of values
we think we have evolved personally, but in reality
are what have been called 'the creation of false
consciousness'.

FALSE CONSCIOUSNESS

The Russian revolutionary, Leon Trotsky (1879 –
1940), spoke of the development of false
consciousness. He meant that through control of
education and the media, in his terms:
'propaganda'[xxiv]- the Establishment pedals invented
'facts', constructed attitudes, values and a morality,
which they impose upon the rest of us.

We, the broad population, the 90% are led to believe
that the Establishment's values and attitudes are

good for us. Eventually, after they are pounded into us in school, through their textbooks, via their corporate fabricated popular culture, by the framing and delivery of 24/7 news, and by the repeated mantras of politicians, we begin to believe that they are actually our own values and attitudes.

After all, they seem to provide our identity, they describe the ties that bind us, and they reassure us, morning after morning, that we have a conventional and therefore safe pattern within life to follow, while actually so many people know that they are frustrated, worn, unhappy and profoundly discontented with life.

The Neoliberal cultural guardians have constructed a new reality that insists on a 'new normal'. We listen to pundits, politicians and celebrities who say little about what we need but say a lot about what we don't need. They fill our minds with hatred or at least suspicion of others, with scorching racism, sexism and nationalism, with avarice and desire for things we have little use for. They taunt us with undeliverable sexual offerings. Whilst they ignore the real needs of our souls, they transform material 'wants' into 'needs' that they propose we can satisfy through consumption of their products and services. They turn us against each other and promote the idea that we are more kindred to a banker of the same religion, colour or nationality than the person working next to us of a different colour who flips the same burgers for the same low wages as do we, while their pundits, politicians and celebs ignore love, kindness and the caring of those who have been left with so little.

Their 'new normal' consists of the day-by-day murdering of black, brown and poor people around the globe; it consists of looking away from the indisputable horror of Syria and the Congo and the on-going mutilation of the Palestinian people. It consists of ignoring one billion starving people on our shared earth and the decimation of other species and of the earth itself. It promotes and also denies it promotes policies and ideas that destroy the middle and working classes in the US and the UK, all in the name of rationality, profits and power - their rationality, profits and power. The depth of hypocrisy is not fathomable.

Generally we do not see their menu of cultural stuff, education and the news as propaganda but as 'how it is' or we think of it as 'common sense'.[xxv]

Its purpose is to convince us that their system is the natural order of things whilst it helps the .01% to profit from our labour. This is the goal of false consciousness: to benefit the wealthy and powerful while tricking the rest of us into accepting political, cultural and economic beliefs that hold us in willing servitude through ignorance, fear and desperation, in a system which lacks truth and destroys our collective and individual imaginations.

The essence of the above is that false consciousness convinces us, while it holds us in its grip, to willingly allow the .01% to excessively exploit our labour for their wealth. It always holds out the figment of class mobility, which hints that through our hard work we too will be able to rise to the top.

This exploitation of labour has existed throughout history, ever since humans began to farm their food, thus liberating some labour from the need to feed the group to become able to specialise in other productive activity like throwing pots, baking bread or brewing hooch. Although capitalism took this to new, more methodical heights of exploitation, since 1980, the greed of the Neoliberals has hugely increased the violence and grasping they are willing to use against the rest of us to enrich themselves.

THREE TOOLS OF CONTROL

Most rulers, ruling classes and parties and most states have sustained their power throughout history by using three forms of control.

They are:
1. convincing the mass of people to accept the belief system imposed upon them from above which serves only the powerful and the wealthy, often referred to as 'manufacturing consent',[xxvi]
2. buying off essential workers,
3. and if all else fails, using violence, legally approved or not, to suppress the people.

The system, even within democracies, is ultimately run on the raw rump of repression, of the biggest guys in the room - usually representatives of the state or a party controlled by criminals, or a class or religious or tribal interests - having the largest clubs. To understand this is to realise that behind all the Democratic tinsel are the state's or group's bullies.

Think of how unnecessarily violent the authorities were with the Occupy and Anti-Globalization movements; remember the on-going cold blooded murders of black people in the US; the violence used to subdue indigenous Americans defending their tribal lands against the oil corporations; recall the number of black people who die in British police custody or the overwhelming numbers of British police used to destroy the miner's resistance at Battle of Orgreave in 1984; or the impatient macho insistence of ending the Waco siege in which 76 people, including unarmed women and children, were killed. This over-reaction indicates the fragility and oppressiveness of the system.

Herbert Marcuse, the German social philosopher mentioned earlier, whose theories influenced the American radical student movements of the nineteen-sixties, wrote a book called *Repressive Tolerance* in which he argued that American democracy has aspects of repression not unlike totalitarian states. In action, this meant that, for instance, the policing of American black communities is always present, always pressing, always reminding people of the watchful state and its power.[xxvii]

ART AND THE IMMORAL BALANCE

However all the above are explained away, however legalistically and reasonably they are rationalised, in the end, balancing the rights of the .01% – which is another way of saying 'the rights of property'[xxviii] against starvation, hunger, illness, unemployment, the impoverishment of billions, against dangerous and poor working conditions, against endless wars, and on and on into our long shared night, none of their words nor explanations make sense.

There is no moral balance between the .01%'s rights to acquire huge wealth and the suffering of billions of others.

Vaclav Havel, (1936-2011) the inspiring Czech intellectual whose resistance, with others, led to the fall of the Communist empire in central Europe, spoke about how they confronted the Soviet terror machine inside Czechoslovakia: *"the more we did, the more we were able to do, and the more we were able to do, the more we did"*. This is a very simple and practical guide for action and possible change.

As always, the moral choices for such a guide are central to the nature of change. He said: *"you act not to receive a certain outcome, you act because it is right."* I believe to be truly heroic it is not only right but also necessary to challenge all of our beliefs, and to plan and create within us and with our neighbour's real and substantial changes that will benefit everyone. This refers to my earlier mention of Marcuse when he talked about the creation of a radical subjectivity. Haval also created the phrase, *"the complete freedom of truth"*. This implies that without complete freedom, we cannot grasp the truth, and without truth we cannot gain complete freedom. What else would anyone want, even if they do not know this? And what else would an artist wish to work for, if not this?

Unless we understand the need for generosity, the need to include everyone in the process of change, unless we say we want all people to share in the good and just life, we will simply give birth to another unfair and oppressive system.

The means do not justify the ends. If you corrupt your struggle, if you accede to violence, immorality and injustice, what you give birth to will have those seeds within it; seeds, which under the right conditions bear poisonous fruits.

What Havel said of his fellow intellectuals is, to my mind, true for art and artists. We must be conscious, we must question and reject the status quo and we must be willing to pick up the lantern, shedding light on the truth, helping to point out the direction where hope will be found.

Artists need to engage with their community; they need to represent the needs and wants of that community for their work to be relevant; they need to describe in whatever poetic way they can, that which arouses, inspires and offers hope. They need to see that their clarity and commitment to change will communicate with others if the work is truthful and good enough; that it will come to offer inspiring archetypes, it will provide ways of acting and thinking, and it will wake people up to their own humanity, reminding them that we are all one.

The sense of oneness makes it difficult to not care about others suffering from wars and privation in distant places. This is how art helps to curb the worst in us.

This is what art and artists can do in these difficult times.

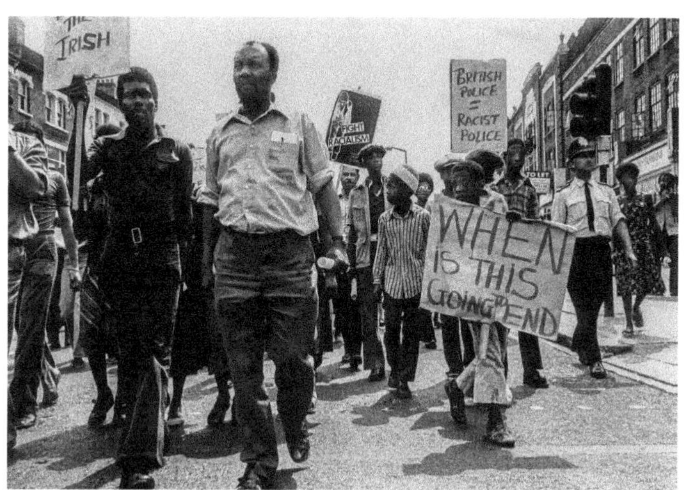

March on the local police station, Willesden, London, 1978;
photograph: Robert Golden

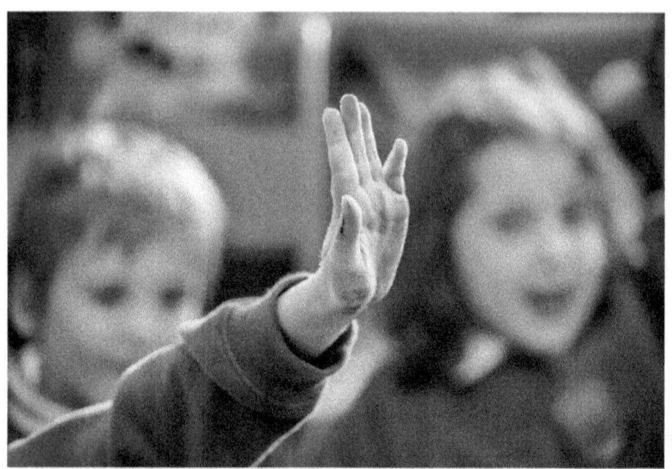

Hand raised in class, Bridport Dorset, March 2014;
photograph, Robert Golden

5
A DREAM

ART AS REDEMPTION

We have been failed by politics, economics, ideology and religion. The only redemptive activity we possess, other than directly helping others, is within culture: creations of the imagination capable of transforming inaction into action, despair into hope, the mundane into beauty, and to share this with our fellow humans.

In this creation we help others to realise that we are like them, that we too, across race, religion, gender, generations and languages, can see and touch each other's souls through beauty, while remembering that for beauty to exist it must embody truth.

One reason many Jewish artists and intellectuals chose suicide when trapped between the Nazis and the Pyrenees Mountains was that they felt isolated, utterly alone, forsaken by the rest of Europe. Art helps people in despair, desperate to recognise that they are not alone and that someone (an artist) somewhere understands and cares about their fate.

ART AND TRANSFORMATIONS

This is a dream: that many and I as well, find ways with our creativity to actively and effectively change people's awareness and therefore their desire to make a kinder, fairer, peaceful and humane world which celebrates, day-by-day, knowledge, beauty and love.

Part of our job is to understand why our masters are continually cruel. What is it that allows them to believe that to do what they do is acceptable? Since Reagan and Thatcher and the inclusion of neoliberal thinking into the bowels of government, many members of the working class through the upper middle classes have been led to accept that avarice is normal and socially acceptable. Turning one's back on the less fortunate, on the victims of imperialist wars, on those who, for whatever reasons, have fallen low has become morally acceptable.

This represents darkness in the souls of the middle classes who would rather accept anti-humane Capitalist practices that may enrich them than say '*no*' to injustice. The media corporations, the school systems and the news, all tightly controlled by the dominant ideology of neoliberalism, have successfully trained two generations into believing that they too can become super wealthy and live a life unaffected by the troubles of the 'less successful'.

As a consequence much of what is judged to be acceptable art has become increasingly preoccupied with autobiographic responses and dead-end formal concerns rather than the lives of others. These contradictions are within the heart of our present social tragedy.

Some artists choose to or must work alone. It should not be a viewer's concern about how the artist works but what they make and whose needs their work represents and how their art is able to communicate things which are at the centre of people's traumas,

struggles and their need for change, but most of all, their need to find freedom.
The preoccupation with artist's processes is the intellectually lazy and emotionally cowardly act of placing form above content. That placement helps to preoccupy the public with the mechanism of making art rather than its content.

Tina Ellen Lee, the artistic director of a British charity which produces operas and runs programmes to help young people discover their leadership capabilities by engaging in the arts, and I have worked in India, Thailand and Vietnam, and for 10 years on and off in Srebrenica and now in the UK using the arts informally as a means to help people find their voices and to overcome social tensions and alienation. It works.

The wonderful thing is that the process actually creates unity between people previously alienated and suspicious of each other, it fosters dreams of something better, it motivates a permanent revolution in people's souls and helps them to travel to emotional and intellectual places previously out of bounds for them, and they often create surprising and profoundly moving work.

This is not a process in which we pander to the canon of the Establishment's culture. We offer something thoughtful and profound – aspirations for meanings that are universal, rather than shards of the infantilized popular culture, which is produced, promoted and sold by the media and the entertainment corporations.

Many people have argued that we need to go to where the children and young people find themselves emotionally and culturally. Unfortunately they are often a result of oppressive schooling and the limiting, infantilizing corporation produced culture that had so deeply disaffected them. We create a safe, free area where they can accept what is on offer from the artists, music makers and others who are there to assist them to develop as they can and may.

Many of the young participants find that being in a truly free environment is an experience so rare in their lives that for several days they find themselves in a kind of culture shock. They only emerge when they recognize that they must make decisions for themselves or with their peers.

There are many consequences to this transformation in people through art: they gain self-respect and a sense of pride and dignity; they realize that their voices count and that what they do helps others to overcome isolation and fear; and it creates a sense of unity between artists and there audiences, an exchange which travels in both directions. It encourages within the new artist a sense of performing a generous duty for their community and awakens notions of neighbourliness, social responsibility and helps to balance their sense of self with that of others. Their community becomes proud of their own friends, neighbours and children aspiring and reaching for beauty. They know that somehow it is right that this should happen.

THE NEED TO FREE ONE'S SELF
FROM THE ESTABLISHMENT

A part of my dream is that people discover true and lasting freedom.

If artists are aware of the unjust system we in the West live within, no matter how humane their intentions, ultimately even they will produce work whilst sitting atop the hideous exploitation and murderous behaviour of the establishment. Thus it is a choice to join with or stand against them. *'Joining with'* means turning a blind eye; *'standing against'* means choosing a very difficult road allowing one to live in truth and to produce meaningful work. This defines whether their art will have lasting meaning or be assigned to the decorative arts and entertainment waste heaps.

I have heard many good and well intended young artists and others claim that immersing themselves in institutions or bureaucracies, that is, associating with those who have power and are on the inside of the establishment, is the way to bring change. This 'deep-enterism' has, for many years, been an argument that to bring change to the status quo one can only do so by affecting the means and methods of the institutions themselves from the inside.

Perhaps it is so that one could turn a head or affect a conscience for a moment, but it ignores the over-arching poisonous embrace, seduction and sheer obduracy of the institutions and the institutionalised. No one who has ever had contact with large state or private institutions or with bureaucrats would accuse them of being sensitive, caring, empathic or imaginative. These four qualities are indispensible to create art.

David Mamet, the American playwright and film-maker wrote,

> *"You will encounter in your travels folks of your own age who chose the institutional path, who became the arts administrators rather than the writers. These folks chose to serve an institutional authority in exchange for a pay-check, and these folks are going to be with you for the rest of your life, and you actors and writers and people who come up off the street, who live without certainty day to day and year to year are going to have to bear with being called children by these institutional types...It is not childish to live with uncertainty, to devote oneself to a craft rather than a career, to an idea rather than an institution. It's courageous and requires a courage of the order that the institutionally co-opted are ill equipped to perceive. They are so unequipped to perceive it that they can only call it childish, and so excuse their exploitation of you."*

For a moment let us think about what distinguishes bureaucracies and large institutions (museums, galleries) that currently manage the outer ideologically fortified walls of the status quo.

> *"Bureaucracy in most cases is about fulfilling a narrow task and passing it on in a hierarchical system to the next office."*

According to Max Weber, one of the founders of
modern sociology, all bureaucratic systems
discourage individual thought including curiosity
and emotional responses. Bureaucracies are soul
destroyers. Bureaucracy is firmly rooted in the past –
a past devoted to maintaining the status quo. For
these reasons, creativity is anathema to its operations.

Bureaucracies are hierarchical to the point of being
dictatorial, often paternalistic, sexist and racist. In
practical terms they are very conservative and wary
of decision-making that could threaten significant
social change. They are managed by terrified people
whose last decision determine their future prospects;
they are staffed by terrified people who fear being
noticed for some difference or perceived lack of
performance. The staff's poor wages ensure they are
always in debt (a form of wage slavery) and
therefore forced into docility for fear of losing home,
possessions and status if fired.

The upper management are almost always tasked
with three things: to continually reduce costs -
meaning to freeze wages, to reduce staff numbers
and to find ways to not fulfil their supposed
responsibilities to the public or their customers and
clients if they can further save money. The
annihilation of emotional responses and intellectual
decision-making is a contemporary goal of
managers, to be realised by replacing as many
employees as possible with computers or robots.

John Kenneth Galbraith, the liberal American/
Canadian economist of the mid-twentieth century
wrote that American corporations had gained

control over their employee's social lives,
communities and of course their economic security
in ways that were not unlike Italian fascism.

Further, it is for staff members to do the dirty work
of the corporations and institution's un-democratic
leadership: turning people away, reducing their
benefits, denying them treatment, delaying their
papers, and everyday practicing their role of
excluding humanity and individuality from the
spaces between the 'yes' and 'no' boxes, while
helping to create a world which only consists of
black or white, ones or zeros. Is it any wonder that
so many office workers suffer from anxiety, guilt,
fragmented personalities, broken dreams, un-
fulfilled desires and frustration?

When it comes to the interface between art and
artists with public and private institutions it is
always about how well-known and accepted the
artist is to the middle classes and to the conservative
media; how their work conforms to that year's
shopping list for the right subject matter and style to
fit into the curator's shelves, and how titillating and
daring it might be within the canon of acceptable
themes and subject matter.

This means that the art can deal with current socially
relevant problems as long as it does not challenge
the status quo in any meaningful way that exposes
the true nature of wealth and power.

Given the above, I have no faith that a trusting,
inexperienced young artist would be able to survive,

thrive and change anything when connected to such
places.

BUILDING ART OUT OF DEMOCRACY

The opposite of the above is the unique relationship
between an artist and the objective world of
appearances. Artists have the ability to transform
three-dimensional kinetic reality into a special kind
of two-dimensional shard of personal and cultural
truths. This is by virtue of their emotional and
intellectual resources that they can transform
objective reality into an expression of their beings. It
is as if their inner nature joins with the outer nature
of other people and things. I am not speaking of
magic, but rather the finest use of their tools,
materials and dreams to represent and feed other's
who hunger for living a more complete life.

Art's toolbox of change can encourage opposition by
offering a vision of a better society. People may
know what to object to, but without a vision of what
they want, they do not know what to put in place of
their oppressor's seductions or enforcements.

If art does not contain seeds of change, then art
contains nothing but forms that are socially
stagnant. What then is possible?

We the people must create viable, humane,
cooperative centres of making, doing and learning
which are owned, operated and run openly with
complete transparency by the community, with
democratic decision-making at its heart. Let the

wisdom, skills, self-interest and foolishness of the people rule.

Vital creativity continues to arise from the poor and working classes because it is they who have the dreams and they who have the greatest need for change. The wealthy only have an interest in holding on to past cultural constructions because their assumptions sustain their wealth; and vast numbers of the middle classes participate in their own oppression because the believe more strongly in the myth of gaining huge wealth, power or station for themselves more than they do in possibilities of creating a better world by turning away from the illusions so convincingly sold by the Establishment.

CREATIVE ROOMS

A part of my dream, as I am sure it is of others, is to create in every neighbourhood, town and village a centre of creative work – music, theatre, fine arts, poetry, spoken word, photography and film-making, cultural analysis, viewing movies, dancing, making music and exhibitions and reading to each other.

We need to motivate young artists to work with older artists – skilled in the ways of suggesting rather than leading – as if a new Peace Corp but of local people. They would be cultural creative beehives gathering people to them.

Recently I tried to organise an afterschool centre for the practice of the arts with young people. It would have been a place where they were safe to experiment and could spend time thinking, doing, working and reworking projects surrounded by equipment, materials, good food and artist/guides to help them, to excite them and to introduce them to the arts, techniques and the life of ideas. I called the project The Creative Rooms.

Sadly I found the institutions we applied to for money had what seemed endless temporal and other requirements to be met which had little to do with a place of nurturing and a lot to do with meeting specific and conventional educational goals and paranoia sponsored bureaucratic rules.

Every grant was short termed expecting to see change within a year, whereas we understood we needed ten years to bring real change to a community. Even more revealing was how petty and closed so many middleclass people were while protecting their own turf, refusing to donate time or money, and revealing how dreamless they were about a project which was not interested in turning a profit or creating entrepreneurs. Only a handful of artists were supportive of the ideas. Alas, others will find ways to do this.

They and others could create catalogues of beauty only surpassed by love. They could decide with the town council to ban all visual advertising to replace it with reproductions of the young people's own and other's inspired art, things to challenge the passers-by. The Rooms would become cradles of exciting ideas where, contrary to the Anglo-American school systems, the children could learn to think and to discover what freedom and democracy really mean.

Yo Yo Ma, the fine musician wrote,
 *"Music is the prism through which I found
the code to strangers' inner lives and learned
to trust them as neighbours. Bluegrass took me
to the American heartland, Piazzolla's tangos
to Argentina, Shostakovich into the Stalinist
era, a blind Namibian musician into the world
of pre-agricultural hunter gatherers, a long
song singer into the heart of Mongolia, and the
poetic aspirations of two young musicians in
Amman, Jordan, led me to Silk Road, a project
that changed how I think about tradition,
music and boundaries. Today, I feel at home in
the world."*

However we accomplish this and whom-so-ever does it, we need to embrace our young and our broader communities within democratic spaces where people do not have to deliver for social worker's projects but rather are able to learn or re-learn to imagine and to create, to reflect their inner wants and needs and to see how they may represent those of their community. Many people understand instinctively that we need a village to raise and educate our children, to care for the elders and to find emotional and intellectual support for everyone.

Culture and the arts in particular can help people understand that to be truly free they must apprehend the realities of their conditions. To be able to be truthful they must be free, and for the moment we only have the arts to lead us their. If this does not happen, when this pernicious neoliberal capitalism fails again, the political vacuum will be filled by racist nationalistic macho militaristic ranting of the populist right, unless artists have done their share in creating an alternative humanised democratic populist alternative in which people can regain the rightful voice promised by the very name Democracy - the people's voice.

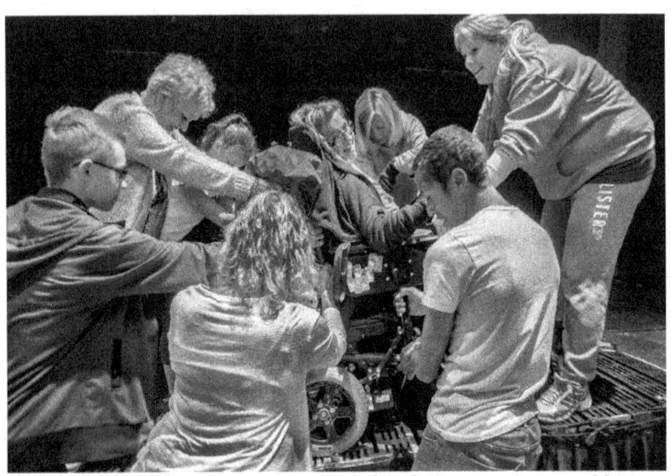

Helping Abi off stage, Bryanston School, Dorset, August 2014;
photograph: Robert Golden

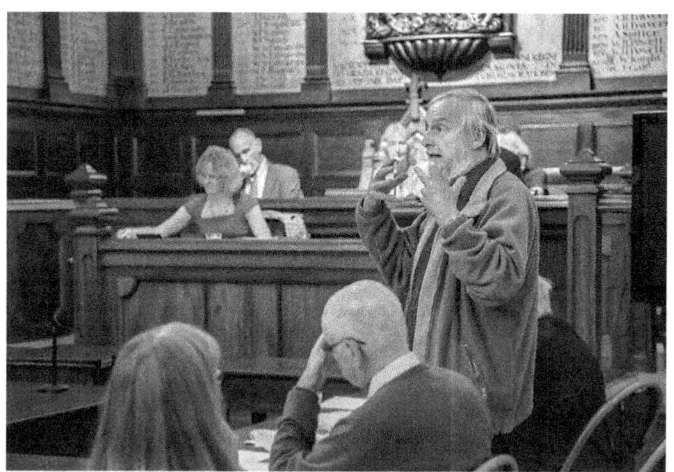

Councillor Dave Rickard speaking at a town council meeting; Bridport, Dorset, Oct 2013; photograph: Robert Golden

ROBERT GOLDEN'S BIOGRAPHIC DETAILS

EDUCATION
Robert Golden was educated at Monteith Collage, in Detroit, Michigan, studying intellectual history for which he was nominated as a Woodrow Wilson Scholar. He graduated University of Michigan with a BA in Modern European History and a BS in Design. He also attended the London School of Film Technique.

PHOTOGRAPHY
In his early career he worked with many magazines and newspapers, creating photo-essays and stories for articles. He was commissioned to photograph well-known actors, politicians and others, producing magazine, book and record covers. He pioneered a new style of advertising and editorial food photography; conceived and shot ten award winning books called the '*People Working Series*' published by Penguin; a book about unemployment called *Down The Road*, and was a major contributor to *The American Air And Space* and the *Natural History Museum* catalogues.

He became Chairman of the Association of Photographers and created the Association Awards, which have since become the most well-known and respected photography awards in Britain for which he received the Chairman's Award in 1996.

He has trained several well-known photographers: Fay Godwin, Eamonn McCabe, and Robin Broadbent.

His stills photographs have been exhibited at:
The Half Moon Gallery/ London (one person show)
The Serpentine Gallery/ London
The Photographer's Gallery/ London (one person show)
The Midland Group Gallery/ GB
The Side Gallery /Newcastle (one person show)
The Hayward Gallery/ London
Victoria and Albert Museum/ London
Barbican Concourse/London (one person show)
The First Georgian State Film and Theatre Festival/Georgia
(one person show)

Battersea Art Centre (theatre works)/London (one person show)
The White Space/ Dorset (one person show)
Greenham Common Gallery/GB (one person show)
The Study Gallery for Modern Art/ Poole, Dorset (one person show)
The Silk Mill for the Frome Festival / Frome, Somerset (one person show)
Bridport Art Centre/ Dorset (one person show)
And had semi-permanent exhibition of still life work at the Lighthouse in Poole Dorset and numerous art centres and galleries around Britain.

MOVING IMAGES

His first feature film, BEG! shared the Audience Award at the Edinburgh Film Festival, and was selected for the Sundance Film Festival amongst other festivals. He has written and filmed 40 documentaries concerned with culture, the arts and social/political problems, winning awards and seen by millions of people around the world, and he's made over 900 commercials for TV as a director/DOP.

For his commercial work he won 3 Cannes Lions, a New York Film and TV Award, many other awards especially in Italy and has been featured in Spots, Campaign and other advertising media.

He wrote and directed a documentary called Candles Against The Night, about a group of teenagers in Srebrenica living in the shadow of genocide, struggling to make a life through cultural engagement.

His documentaries have won several awards and have been selected for numerous Festivals around the world. Another film, called A Gift Of Culture has been shown in many universities and also at the Davos Economic Forum. He recently finished a film about Bridport Dorset's Literary and Science Institute called THE PROMISE and has several other films in research and production.

WRITING

Robert had written 3 plays, a poetry cycle, a novel, an epic poem directed by him for the theatre, 8 feature film scripts, 40 documentary scripts, 2 books about photography and another about unemployment. He has also illustrated over 30 cookery and other books.

He has written many essays on photography and on issues about regional food sustainability and politics and is currently writing a set of essays called WHY?

His first novel, A Forgettable Man, about a photojournalist has been published to excellent reviews and he is currently working on several films, a second novel called A Vengeful Man and a graphic novel.

WORKSHOPS/TALKS

Robert mentors and is invited to speak increasingly frequently. He has designed a number of different sets of workshops and talks, running from several hours to 10 days, about photography, film-making and storytelling.

CHARITABLE WORK

He was on the board of the Helen Bamber Foundation and supported the Medical Foundation for the Care of Victims of Torture (now Freedom From Torture) for many years.

Over the last 8 years he has worked closely with young people in Srebrenica and other young people from around Europe helping them to workshop film and photography practice and has also worked with the European youth project – The Complete Freedom of Truth, running workshops about democracy, neoliberalism and the purpose of art in a challenging world.

He runs Home In Bridport, a charity that serves the community and donates time photographing, filming and designing graphics for various causes.

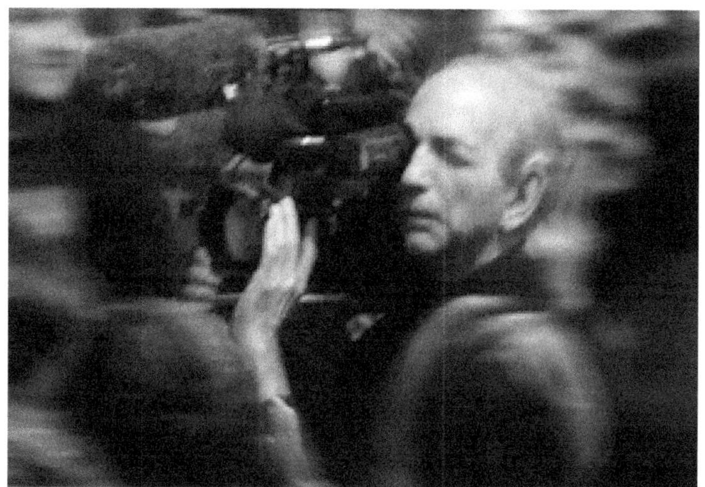

Robert Golden filming in the UK

FOOTNOTES

---

[i] Leonard Cohen wrote in his song *You Want It Darker*
"They're lining up the prisoners and the guards are taking aim.
I struggle with some demons they were middle class and tame
and I didn't know I had permission to murder and to maim."

[ii] The Establishment can be counted as those with power
in the media and entertainment industries, the financial
markets, corporations and institutions of the state
including the big bureaucracies, and the upper ranks of
the army, secret services and police. They comprise about
10% of the society.

[iii] English Studies Department, Université Bordeaux-Montaigne,
Bordeaux, France.

[iv] A magazine dedicated to discussing photography's role
in society.

[v] Ben Okri is a Nigerian poet and novelist, born in 1959.

[vi] In many dictionaries one of the first usages of the word
'consumption' (as in the *New Oxford Dictionary*) is "to
consume by fire."

[vii] The work of Gene Sharp, an American dissenter and
the writer of *From Dictatorship To Democracy*, revealed
through extensive research that peaceful resistance is
twice as likely to succeed in changing society as is
violence. Within this change, creativity and artists play a
vital role.

[viii] 'Quasi art' is a form of creativity that echoes ideological
impositions to deliver the message of a state, a party, a
church or to serve fundamentalist's thinking.
These works silence curiosity and dialogue; they are
simplistic, single dimensional commands that are in fact

propaganda or totalitarians decrees. An example is post revolutionary Soviet 'Art', although constructed of pleasing graphics, was none the less shallow.

[x] Neoliberalism is what it says it is. It is a new liberalism, rather than the old liberalism based on the economic and political ideas of the 18th century Scottish philosopher, Adam Smith. His views were that people, by whom he meant Capitalists, needed to be sufficiently unencumbered by taxes, legislation, tariffs and regulations to allow the 'market' the ability to evolve naturally. He also said that for Capitalism to be successful it needed to create a fair society. Neoliberalism, a new-speak word, means quite the opposite in that it wishes to extract as much profit as possible from the working people, to reduce the size of the state, to have the state represent only capitalist's best interests, and to disinherit all social programmes whilst denying the value of community.

[xi] "Nihilism" comes from the Latin *'nihil'*, or nothing, which means *'not anything'*, *'that which does not exist'*. It appears in the verb *'annihilate'*, meaning *'to bring to nothing'*, *'to destroy completely'*.
Internet Encyclopaedia Of Philosophy

[xii] John Locke, an English philosopher and thinker of the 17th century, is considered the father of Liberalism.

[xiii] John Berger is often mentioned or quoted because, as Albert Camus, George Steiner, Herbert Marcuse and a handful of other philosophers, critics, and poets, they have had a profound influence on my thinking across many years. Berger in particular, in his novels and art criticism, has continually touched my soul and stirred my intellect with his humane, perceptive and unique ways of seeing life and the world.

xiv Albert Camus was an Algerian born French philosopher who fought against the Nazi invasion of France in the underground and was also a novelist, playwright and philosopher.

xv A distorted form of naturalism aggrandizing heroic workers sacrificing themselves for the creation of socialism and the new socialist state, but which was in reality a superficial one-way propagandized monologue exhorting the people to sacrifice their lives to industrialize mother Russia overnight.

xvi Humanist instincts stand against war and for equality, kindness and democratic institutions.

xvii I know that when a 1 inch cube of lead is raised to 3200 degrees Kelvin, the colour of its glow will be orange. I believe that the 99% of scientists who say that climate change is in large part a consequence of human activity are correct. I hope that what I am saying today does approach shared objective, universal truths.

xviii Benjamin Barber was an American cultural commentator best know for his book *Jihad Vs Mcworld*.

xix "They decided"...the Neoliberals decided to create this new system of economics, politics and culture.

xx Chomsky and Herman clearly outlined the need for these larger organizations in that the investment in technology and the on-going development of programming needed significant amounts of capital. These corporations were almost entirely dependent on advertising. Since corporate America wishes to not only sell their wares but also wish to instil false consciousness.

xxiThis brainwashing is a consequence of the insistent repetition of the same 'Big Lie' via the news cycle, politician's sound bites, and notions sewn into the fabric of popular culture, schoolbooks and the general education. Soon the Big Lie becomes a part of our belief system, our common knowledge – that which we accept as part of the explanation of our world – as for instance, the overwhelming importance of the number representing the Gross Domestic Product and therefore a supposed accurate indication of our relative wellbeing in that year.

[xxii] Eugene O'Neill was an American playwright of the early to mid 20th century who introduced his audiences to European realism.

[xxiii] The beliefs that form the cultural canon are a set of rules, norms and ideas acceptable to representatives of the Fraternity. Although mostly unknown to us, it represents the interests of the ruling powers. It helps them to control the 90% in the least expensive way by instilling a belief system and sets of values that do a good job at convincing us that the current political/economic relations are the natural order of things.

[xxiv] Propaganda offers a one-sided point of view, delivered with no regard for facts, careful analysis or balancing a pluralistic point of view. It is an instrument to convince people to accept the ideology of the party, the leader or the state. In Western culture, much of what we are continually exposed to is so tightly controlled that pluralism, which allows for alternative points of view, is permitted neither access nor air time in the popular media. Many political campaigns are run on the basis of slight differences, personality traits and preferences, and outright lies. Almost never do we hear a real alternative.

[xxv] John Berger described common sense as *'a homemade ideology of those who have been deprived of fundamental learning, of those who have been kept ignorant.'*

xxvi *Manufacturing Consent* is the title of a book written by Chomsky and Herman.

xxvii US repression in the earlier part of the 20th century took the form of arresting young black men on the grounds of vagrancy and since the 1980s, arrests and intimidation have taken place within the so called 'war on drugs,' leading to the greatest number of people being incarcerates as a proportion of any country's total population.

xxviii I wish, as I suppose most of us do, to believe in the American Myth and the British Spirit of '45 - that the Declaration of Independence of 1776, the *Constitution of the United States* in 1783 and the *Bill of Rights* were written with all of us in mind, manifesting the best that the Founding Fathers could offer. It is like a dose of salts to read further into the history to discover that most of those present were either well-to-do lawyers or large landowners whose interests were to maintain their wealth while getting on-side as many white property owning men as they could during their anti-British, anti-imperial war so that they would replace the British as rulers of America.

Howard Zinn, the historian, quotes the findings of an earlier historian: "…in 1687, there were, out of a population of six thousand (in Boston), about one thousand property owners, and the richest 1 percent of the whole population consisted of 50 rich individuals who possessed 25 percent of the wealth. By 1770, the top 1 percent of property owners owned 44 percent of the wealth."

Whose wealth, whose land did they own and how did they get it? First from massacring the local tribes by bribing or forcing the local armed farmers and the British troops to commit heinous crimes, and then by using their new wealth to control the poor tenant farmers and local craftsmen via their ownership of land and buildings, and finally through loans and then the exploitation of slaves and indentured servants.

Although legal status has changed for some – that slavery was finally outlawed, that women and un-propertied men were allowed the vote, but now there are new forms of servitude and enslavement through bank lending, referred to as 'debt slavery'.

Even more upsetting is to realise that all of the talk of fairness regarding property has been written to defend the landlord against the tenant, the banker against the borrower, the corporation against its workers and consumers, the insurance company against the insured and the government against the governed.

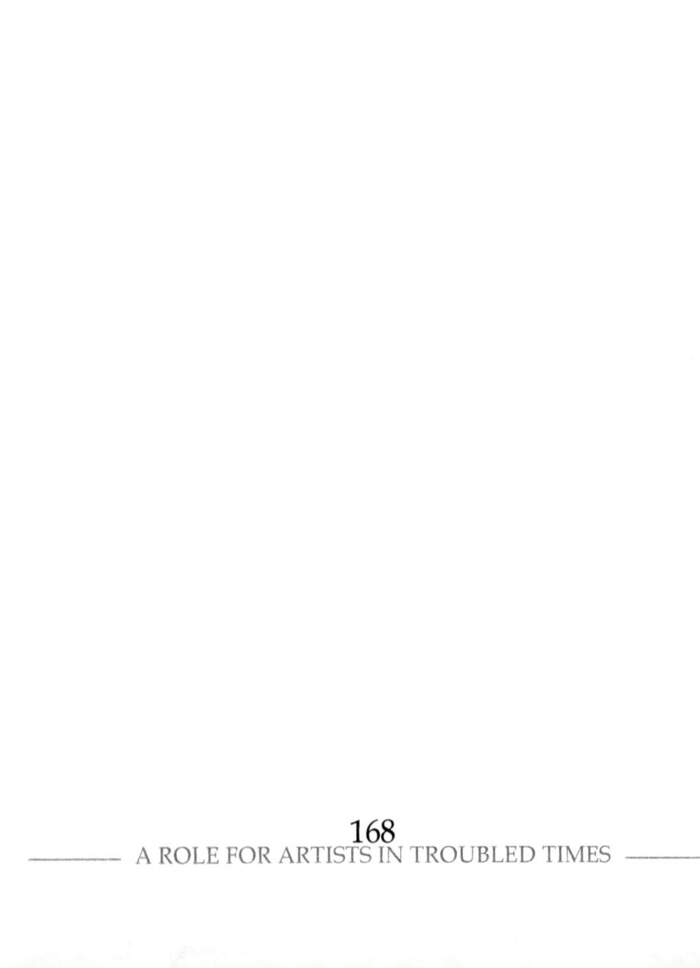